TOO
MUCH

Also by Terri Cole

Boundary Boss

The Boundary Boss Workbook

TOO MUCH

A GUIDE TO BREAKING THE CYCLE OF HIGH-FUNCTIONING CODEPENDENCY

TERRI COLE

sounds true
BOULDER, COLORADO

Sounds True
Boulder, CO

This book is not intended as a substitute for the medical recommendations of physicians,
mental health professionals, or other health-care providers. Rather, it is intended to offer
information to help the reader cooperate with physicians, mental health professionals,
and health-care providers in a mutual quest for optimal well-being. We advise readers to
carefully review and understand the ideas presented and to seek the advice of a qualified
professional before attempting to use them.

For the sake of privacy and confidentiality, all of the case examples are composites of
individuals rather than the story of any one particular person. All names have been
changed to protect their privacy.

Published 2024

Book design by Charli Barnes

Printed in Canada

BK06791

Library of Congress Cataloging-in-Publication Data

Names: Cole, Terri, author.
Title: Too much : a guide to breaking the cycle of high-functioning codependency / by
    Terri Cole.
Description: Boulder, CO: Sounds True Inc., 2024. | Includes bibliographical references.
Identifiers: LCCN 2024006727 (print) | LCCN 2024006728 (ebook)
    | ISBN 9781649631862 (hardback) | ISBN 9781649631879 (ebook)
Subjects: LCSH: Codependency.
Classification: LCC RC569.5.C63 C65 2024 (print) | LCC
    RC569.5.C63 (ebook) | DDC 362.29/13--dc23/eng/20240408
LC record available at https://lccn.loc.gov/2024006727
LC ebook record available at https://lccn.loc.gov/2024006728

FSC
www.fsc.org
MIX
Paper | Supporting
responsible forestry
FSC® C016245

It is my deepest desire that the insights shared within

the pages of this book will lead to your recovery

from the need to do and be everything for everyone

(a.k.a. a high-functioning codependent), as well

as profound self-acceptance and inner peace.

It is through surrender and presence that you will

create a life more spectacular and satisfying than your

wildest dreams. This life awaits you. I am honored

to be your guide on this transformational journey.

To my devoted husband, Victor Juhasz.

None of this happens without your unwavering

support and unending patience. I love you the most.

To my mom and sisters who lovingly permitted

me to share our collective stories.

Contents

Contents

Introduction

YEARS AGO, I was standing on the train platform on my way home from seeing my therapist in Long Island when a skinny kid holding a blanket caught my eye. My helper radar pinged. *Huh,* I thought. *Wonder what his deal is.*

Once we boarded the train, I started chatting with him. Turns out, Billy had been scheduled to drive a car across the country, but at the last minute, the job got canceled, and now he was stranded, heading to New York City, a place he'd never been, with nowhere to sleep.

Billy, who was probably about nineteen years old, looked especially naïve. At twenty-three, I wasn't exactly world-weary, but I did live and work in New York City. Keep in mind, it was the late eighties and the city was still rough. Surely, I could help.

"Wait, so what are you going to do?" I asked him.

"Sleep in the station, I guess," he replied nonchalantly.

"Which station?"

"Penn Stati—"

"No," I said, interrupting him. "You *cannot* sleep in Penn Station. You'll get mugged. You're coming home with me."

So that's how I came to bring a perfect stranger home to my studio apartment, which I shared with a friend. I didn't even bother to stop and call her to see if she minded. I figured she'd agree that we could not let poor Billy face the wilds of New York City on his own, and I was correct.

Years later, I see the Billy story as emblematic of what used to be an everyday occurrence for me—making other people's issues and problems, even strangers', *my* responsibility. Prioritizing the wants, needs, and outcomes of others over my own well-being was my default setting. *Must. Help. Everyone.*

Fortunately, Billy was harmless and left the next morning without incident. But that doesn't mean my over-functioning, hyper-responsible behavior wasn't problematic. Today, what stands out most to me is how compulsive I was in deciding that *I* needed to save him. There was a complete lack of space between my thoughts, feelings, and actions. Immediately, I'd said, "That's it, you're coming with me." It never occurred to me to pause and consider, *Hmmm...is this even my problem to solve?*

I had other options, of course. I could have given Billy the name of a hostel or suggested he plant himself somewhere safer than Penn Station. I could have pulled out five bucks so he could get some coffee and a snack. Or, I could have minded my own damn business.

Instead of exercising any of these options, I projected my worst fears onto Billy (who seemed totally okay with his plans) and instantly made this projection more important than my own well-being (and my roommate's well-being). The truth is, I was used to operating this way in all areas of my life, with loved ones, coworkers, and yes, even strangers.

While you may not have gone to the extreme lengths I did with Billy, perhaps you have your own version of veering out of your own lane and taking the helm of someone else's decisions and life because you feel a deeply ingrained responsibility for others.

Consider the following:

- Are you often the person that people come to for advice or when they are in a jam?

- Do you regularly accommodate others' needs and preferences?

- Do you ever say yes to avoid an issue when you want to say no?

- Do you over-give and receive less in return?

- Are you a professional "fixer," always on, always ready to act on behalf of others?

- Are you so highly capable that it sometimes feels like if you don't handle the travel plans / organize the calendar / divvy up the check at group dinners / solve your babysitter's family drama / sort out your bestie's existential crisis that chaos will ensue?

If any of the above questions resonate, the odds are good that you are one of my over-functioning, over-giving, and over-extending sisters. These are common behaviors of codependency, along with too much doing, feeling, managing, directing, leading, convincing, cajoling, and more. My goal in writing this book is to guide you away from *too much* to *just right*, and to help you find a way out of any behavioral patterns that might be draining your energy and causing harm to you and your relationships.

Fortunately, you are in the right place. Not only am I one of you—I have spent the last two decades in recovery from doing "too much"— but as a licensed psychotherapist, teacher, and master coach, I've devoted a great deal of time to learning about the underpinnings of codependency and figuring out how to teach others to unravel the psychological knots that keep us running ragged. I'm passionate about helping women raise their awareness around dysfunctional behavioral patterns and disordered boundaries so they can enact real-deal change every day and live happier, healthier, more peaceful lives.

Change *is* possible. Not only have I experienced this transformation in my own life, but I have also witnessed it in the lives of the countless clients I've treated in my therapy practice and students I've taught in my courses. I've encountered highly-capable women from all walks of life—CEOs and executives, on-the-rise journalists and acclaimed artists, supermoms and super friends. And while each has a unique set of circumstances, most, if not all, have displayed symptoms of codependency. This leaves them feeling exhausted, with limited energy left to devote to their own internal well-being and dreams. Many are driven by the unconscious belief that the weight of the world rests on them—and it's up to them, and them *alone*—to fix what's wrong. Many have spent their days in a state of busyness and low-grade tension, over-functioning and wondering, *Am I the only one who knows how to get anything done around here?* Many eventually reach a tipping point where they feel like life is an endless series of checking boxes, even when they're engaged in activities that used to bring them joy. It can be hard to access joy, inspiration, and hope if you're feeling bogged down by obligation, exhaustion, or frustration, and chronically feeling a bit underappreciated.

If you are nodding your head in recognition, let me reassure you. There *is* a way out of the suffering, one that requires you to become more self-reflective and honest with yourself about what's driving your behavior. Once your self-knowledge increases and you start to have important epiphanies about why you function the way you do, you are in a position to make more mindful choices about how you want to relate. This understanding enables you to create the relationships and life you desire, taking one right action after another.

There's no cure for codependency, but there is recovery. In recovery, you notice when you're tempted to fall back into dysfunctional behaviors—which includes disordered boundaries—but have the awareness to choose differently. So, as you read through this book, please be patient with yourself.

Many of us were conditioned to be outwardly focused on the wants, desires, needs, and comfort of other people—to be caretakers. We learned to do whatever we needed to avoid negative feedback from the grown-ups in our life. We may struggle with disappointing others because we're still operating with and driven by a childhood fear of rejection and judgment. First, it came from our parents or caregivers, and then it was reinforced by our teachers, friends, bosses, and coworkers. And then those messages were repeated and reinforced by culture, in television shows and movies, on social media, and every corner of society, really. Over and over, we're told that being kind, generous, nice, and self-sacrificing is desirable, and that considering our own needs, wants, and priorities makes us self-absorbed, dramatic, or mean. So, it's no wonder that in adulthood we compulsively shift into over-functioning and hyper-responsibility. These behavioral patterns are highly programmed and largely unconscious.

The solution is simple—it is not easy, but it *is* simple. By learning to distinguish what's your responsibility and what isn't (or what's your side of the street and what's not, as I often put it), the process of transformation becomes much more accessible and straightforward. Your ultimate success comes from your willingness to be open to new ways of relating to yourself, which will positively impact the way you relate to others and the world at large.

Stepping out of an ingrained mindset and behaviors can feel daunting at times, especially in the beginning of recovery. That's normal. However, if you remain dedicated to the practice of staying on your side of the street, you will definitely see results. This requires diligence. You wouldn't expect to become fluent in a different language by going to one class. This is the same, and here, too, your commitment is worth it. By the time you are done reading this book, you are going to know yourself in a more real and intimate way—resulting in less stress, more ease, and better-quality relationships, especially the relationship you have with yourself.

So, let's get to it. Here's an overview of what we'll be covering in *Too Much*. In chapter 1, we'll explore the term "codependency," its origins, and how I expanded its definition to fit our modern lives based on a specific set of behaviors I witnessed repeatedly in my therapy practice of over twenty-five years. (But listen up if you're already shrinking away from the idea of codependency. What matters much more than the *label* is identifying your habits and conditioning so that you can heal and live your best life.) For the rest of part 1, we'll be identifying problematic behaviors and raising your awareness of how you relate to yourself and others. To align your behavior with your true desires, we're going to be spending some time clearing out what I refer to as your "basement"—in other words, your unconscious mind. We'll be looking at your relationship blueprint, which reflects the messages you received in early life—from family, your community, and society—around how to relate to others. So, yes, we will be taking a walk down memory lane to examine how these early influences are impacting your current life, in service of redesigning your blueprint so that it reflects your desires and values. The goal of this process isn't to cast blame on anyone, like your parents or caregivers, but to support you in living the self-determined, sovereign, and joyful life that you deserve. Rest assured that you will be carefully guided throughout the process. Take breaks whenever you need to. This process moves at your pace and according to your readiness.

Part 2 is focused on changing how you relate to yourself and the world, helping you stay centered in your own experience so that you can engage with others in a healthier way. We'll cover relational experiences in your adult life that are still being fueled by unresolved injuries or issues from the past (because disconnection puts you in prime position to backslide into dysfunctional behaviors), and learn how to stay present anytime an interaction creates an uncomfortable emotional charge. We'll also cover how to handle relapses, which can happen especially in times of crisis, and examine potential reactions from those who have grown accustomed to your self-abandoning, overly accommodating ways. You'll get strategies for weathering a period of discomfort where you're beginning to make positive changes but haven't yet mastered your new, life-affirming skill set. Knowledge is power, and throughout this book, you will receive important intel for making lasting behavioral changes, which benefits everyone, including and especially *you*.

How to Use This Book

Whatever your reading style, take note that this book is designed to be consumed in chronological order, as each chapter builds on the one before it. To help you apply what you're learning, I offer tips, self-assessments, and exercises throughout each chapter. These are the same things I use with my clients and students, and they are essential to achieving your desired results.

Here's what you'll find in every chapter:

Say It with Me: Powerful, positive statements designed to help you reframe your mindset and boost your self-esteem. Use them as affirmations to guide your thoughts and actions.

Loving Reminder: Heartfelt messages and insights that serve as gentle nudges, reminding you of the importance of your journey and the power of self-love.

Check In: Moments of introspection to help you reflect on your journey, offering a space to personalize the insights and apply them to your life.

Back to You: Quick, on-the-fly self-assessments to help you personalize and internalize the encouraging self-discovery information and apply it immediately to your unique experiences.

Take Action: At the end of each chapter, *Take Action* sections present practical exercises and actionable steps.

- **Top of Mind:** Helpful ways to expand your self-awareness and keep your personal growth journey at the forefront of your thoughts.

- **Take Care:** Emphasizes the importance of self-care, providing guidance on incorporating nurturing practices into your daily routine.

- **Go Deeper:** Directs you to the back of the book, where you'll find more in-depth self-awareness exercises and prescriptions, allowing you to tailor your healing journey.

You can also grab an HFC Bonus Bundle online. Get exclusive mindfulness tools, guided meditations, and supplemental strategies at hfcbook.com/resources.

This book is a journey of self-discovery and empowerment, and I encourage you to engage with each section fully to reap the greatest benefits. If you like to take notes, you might want to keep a journal handy.

My advice? Go at your own pace, take what works, and leave the rest.

If you're familiar with my work from social media, my podcast, *The Terri Cole Show*, one of my online courses, or my book, *Boundary Boss*, you may recognize some of my core teaching concepts throughout the following pages. I have developed these concepts over the past two-plus decades as a therapist, coach, and teacher. Here, the 3Qs for Clarity, Repeating Relationship Realities, Zen Den, and Blueprints will all be covered specifically through the lens of codependency and relational patterns. These are my tried-and-true signature strategies and tools to accelerate your healing process.

As you embark on this healing journey, you may feel some regret or shame for how you've behaved in the past. This is normal. Consider this whole book a no-judgment zone. You're taking stock and gathering data to help you make better choices today and going forward. Being codependent doesn't mean you're a bad person or an intentional control freak. It means that you have some learned behaviors that you might want to unlearn, that's all. Exercising self-compassion is important as you grapple with some of these more entrenched dynamics. *Too Much* raises your awareness and provides an education on healthy relating. As I said above, these dysfunctional behaviors you're working to change were taught to you from the earliest age, and they are not your fault. Self-awareness is our greatest tool for separating healthy behaviors from dysfunctional ones. Once you raise your self-awareness, making desired changes to your precious, one-of-a-kind life becomes possible.

Step by step, you can learn to make small but potent shifts that will result in major relationship breakthroughs, such as saying no when you want to say no, pausing before twisting yourself up into a pretzel for anyone, not putting your roommate in a precarious position by inviting a perfect stranger for a sleepover—and so much more. *Everything* changes when you do.

What you feel *matters*. What you think *matters*. What you want *matters*. In fact, those things need to matter *to you* the most. This may be a new lens with which to view your choices and a little uncomfortable at first. That's okay. Creating sustainable change is going to take some work, but I have no doubt you have what it takes.

By choosing the path of healing and recovery, you are coming home to yourself—perhaps for the very first time. There's great beauty, richness, and reward in this process, so keep your goals in mind if you start to feel overwhelmed. Knowing yourself on these deeper levels means you're creating the opportunity for others to know you more deeply as well. And that's what this life is all about.

I've taught thousands of people worldwide how to create lives that thrill and fulfill them using my proven transformation techniques. This approach is based on self-awareness, self-knowledge, self-compassion, and self-love.

I want that for you too, because you are *it* for me; you are the reason I do what I do.

I am committed to adding value to your life and helping you achieve your dreams and desires. I have written this book for you and believe with all my heart that if you stay the course, it holds the key to your liberation from *too much* to *just right*.

I am so excited to guide you on this transformational and healing journey. Let's GO!!

PART 1

Unhealed HFC

Managing, Meddling, and Over-Functioning

CHAPTER 1

When Doing *Too Much* Is Really Too Much

YEARS AGO, I was in my office on West 22nd Street in New York City, waiting expectantly for Andrea, a successful, middle-aged lawyer who had initially sought therapy to better manage the overwhelming amount of stress she had in her life. Like many of my clients, Andrea was perpetually overscheduled with work, home, and personal obligations. Yet somehow, she always showed up on time for our sessions and with a checklist of talking points. So, I was surprised when she'd canceled at the last minute the week prior. Though she had sent a short text five minutes before the session was to begin, I was concerned by her out-of-character behavior.

At home and in life, Andrea was a consummate *doer*—a doting mom of two high-energy, school-age children, a dutiful spouse, and a reliable relative and friend. Meanwhile, she worked sixty hours a week at the firm and still managed to volunteer at her local community center, chair the parents' committee at her kids' school, and spearhead fun adventures with her circle of tight-knit pals. On top of that, Andrea was the go-to gal for all her loved ones. For anyone who needed advice, perspective, or a shoulder to cry on, Andrea was there, usually with a wry joke, Kleenex, and a clearly outlined plan to fix whatever the issue was. If you're thinking, *How the heck did she have time for all this?* The answer is, *she didn't*. Yet, like so many of my go-getting clients, she persisted, over-extended, and attempted to bend the laws of time and space, insisting everything was "fine." Because, really, if she didn't do all the things, who would? So, she just kept on going.

There were chinks in her armor, though. "Why is everyone so inefficient?" had become a familiar refrain when she came to my office. Her family, her colleagues, her friends, and, well, the world at large, none of them could ever seem to match Andrea's high capability.

Lately, she seemed *extra* irritated about matters large and small, saying things like, "Can you believe Jack just expects *me* to pick up our daughter from her sleepover in the middle of the night?" And, "My friends just assume that I'll be the one to take care of all the travel plans as if I'm the only one who has an Airbnb account." And, "It never even occurred to my law partner to think about making the lunch reservation for our biggest client. Do I have to freakin' do *everything*?"

Whether she *had* to do everything or not, she *was* doing everything. And I wondered if her anger—and growing stress levels, and inability to say no—had anything to do with why she had missed our recent appointment.

In general, Andrea overestimated her bandwidth and energy. She couldn't see the connection between her high level of stress and the amount she was always doing for others. Andrea's relationship with herself was never a part of the equation. *Your business is my business* seemed to be her motto.

So many of us were taught that endlessly saying yes is a badge of honor. This belief shapes our interactions and impacts the quality of our lives. Like most of my high-achieving clients, women who are always ready to handle whatever crisis may be exploding, Andrea knew that logically she *could* say no to her family, her crew, and her coworkers. But in practice? She rarely did.

BACK TO YOU
Take Stock: Are You Doing It All?

Sometimes we don't realize how much we're doing until we take an inventory. Read through the questions below and jot down your answers.

- How many hours a week do you work (inside or outside the home)?

- If you have kids, are you the "default" parent when it comes to taking care of them (meals, school drop-off/pick-up, appointments, activities, PTA meetings, clothing, playdates, etc.)?

- How much time do you invest in staying in touch with family?

- Who does the housework? If it's split, what's the percentage for each person?

- When a friend/relative/family member/coworker needs something, do you drop everything to help them?

- If you are partnered, how much of your partner's life do you manage (think: social, health, fitness, family, work, etc.)?

- Do you stay in touch with your partner's family more than they do?

- How many people are you a confidante to?

As you look over your answers, consider how these aspects of your life are shaping your current reality. Right now, we are in the awareness-raising and information-gathering stage of our journey and not taking any new actions.

"There's No Way I'm Codependent"

When Andrea walked into my office and plopped down on the couch, she let out a long sigh. She had circles under her eyes and wore a semi-wrinkled blouse.

"What happened last week?" I asked.

"Ugh—I was recovering from a trip to the ER the night before," she said. "But don't worry, I'm fine."

"What sent you to the ER?" I asked.

"Well, it all started with an *insane* day at work. A critical deposition went long, putting me behind. My assistant was out sick. And I had to do some internet doctoring for my coworker who had some weird rash on his neck—," she said, rolling her eyes. "*That* was lovely."

Then when she got home, Andrea's ten-year-old daughter was very clingy, and Evelyn, the babysitter, unloaded *her* stress—about her father's illness and her boyfriend's suspected infidelity.

"My God, Terri, all I said to her was a simple, 'How are you?'" Andrea said, still exasperated a week later. "I offered to put her in touch with a doctor friend who might offer ideas on her father's condition. But with the boyfriend, oh, I had some thoughts—"

In the midst of reminding Evelyn of the *last* time her boyfriend stepped out and helping her to figure out a game plan to leave this jerk, Andrea suddenly couldn't breathe.

Her condition became so intense that she wound up in the ER, where a doctor asked, "Have you ever experienced a panic attack before?"

"I felt like an elephant was sitting on my chest. I told them, 'This is definitely not that! I feel like I'm dying!' There's *no* chance in hell that it was just a panic attack."

Well, according to the EKG results, Andrea was not having a heart attack. In fact, she had no heart problems at all. The doctor prescribed rest and suggested she look into stress management techniques.

"Terri, this cannot all be in my head."

Andrea might not have connected the elephant on her chest with her over-functioning (doing all the things for all the people), but her enmeshed (overly involved) style of relating to *everyone* in her life—and beyond—sure seemed like the elephant in the room to me.

"What do you think a panic attack is?" I asked.

"That's when you crack under pressure?"

Time and time again, I'd noticed that women like Andrea, who "do it all," and are intelligent, capable, and hardworking, tended to see anxiety as equaling weakness. *There must be something wrong with me,* they tell themselves.

I assured her, "It's more like when all the pressure you're under finally boils over. And let's be clear: it has nothing to do with your mental fortitude."

Though Andrea harbored a belief that she could handle everything—for her husband, family, friends, clients, *and* support staff—her body was telling a different story. The whispers of her increasing exhaustion had now become a full-fledged crisis. She could no longer deny that something had to give. Andrea's stressful visit to the ER was an invitation to self-awareness—waking her up to her habitual patterns of doing *too much* for others while neglecting her own needs.

She looked at me, then glanced down at the floor.

"The way you're relating to the folks in your life," I ventured, "is codependent."

At the mention of codependency, Andrea's head whipped up.

"*Codependent?* Me?" she said. "Terri, you know I'm not dependent on anyone. Everyone relies on *me*."

This was not the first time I'd had a client reject my observations of codependent behavior. That's because most people, in my professional experience, don't understand what codependency actually *is*.

Myths of Codependency

There's a whole lot of confusion and misconception about codependency. Before we go any further, let's tackle some of the most prevalent myths:

Myth #1: Codependency only occurs in relationships with addicts.

False. While codependency is often present in addict/enabler relationships, it is not the only kind of relationship in which it can show up.

Myth #2: Only women are codependent.

False. Though we usually think of codependency as a women's affliction, any gender or gender expression, including male and male-identifying, binary, and nonbinary folks, can be codependent.

Myth #3: Codependency only happens in romantic relationships.

False. Codependency can happen in *any* relationship dynamic, with family members, coworkers, clients, romantic partners, or friends (shout out to *allllll* the codependent female friendships of my twenties).

Myth #4: Only emotionally weak people are codependent.

False. Codependency has nothing to do with being "weak" or "strong"—and everything to do with *boundaries*. I've seen many strong-willed, confident, and daring women fall into dysfunctional behavioral patterns that were modeled by their earliest caregivers. "Weak" is definitely a misnomer.

Myth #5: You can always spot a codependent.

False. In fact, many people do not identify with the old-school definition of codependency and cannot even spot it within themselves—which is exactly why I wrote this book.

→ CHECK IN

Take a moment to reflect on your current understanding of codependency. How does it align or differ from the myths and explanations provided?

Old-School Codependency

Much of what we understand about codependency today can be traced back to the seventies, when new theories of caretaking, code-pendency, and enmeshed relationships were emerging in the fields of addiction and recovery. For clarity, codependency is not a clinical diagnosis or a personality disorder but it is recognized as a pervasive issue in the mental health field.

The publication of *Codependent No More*, by Melody Beattie, in the mid-eighties popularized the term "codependent" and struck a chord of recognition and relief in women across the world.

In *Codependent No More*, Beattie highlighted the lack of consensus around a clear definition of codependency. Decades later, while many brilliant thinkers have brought nuance and variation to our under-standing of its symptoms and behaviors, the lack of consensus around what codependency is, definitively, remains. That said, most psychol-ogists would agree that people displaying codependent behaviors are overly reliant on and overly invested in others (usually a romantic partner, family member, or BFF) for support, validation, and identity. This over-investment can lead them to automatically, instinctively, and even compulsively organize their life around others, creating lopsided and unhealthy relationships where they sacrifice their own needs to meet the needs of someone else—even if the help is not asked for.

The term *codependency* has evolved since the late eighties and nineties. However, one of the most enduring assumptions about codependent individuals is that they are long-suffering, disempowered women who cannot escape an unhealthy dynamic with their substance-dependent loved one. This assessment is understandable, given that many pioneers in the field of codependency developed their theories within the context of addiction and recovery.

The Reframe:
High-Functioning Codependency (HFC)

Over and over, my therapy clients, like Andrea, balked at my observation of their codependent interactions because they did not see themselves in the old school definition of codependency. And because they didn't see themselves, they dismissed the idea altogether. They were highly capable, successful, and much too "in charge" to be "reliant" or dependent on others.

But I urgently wanted my clients to be able to identify the disordered relational patterns that were causing their pain. Only then could they stop the behaviors that were pushing them to the point of exhaustion and resentment. Without that identification, the path to healing was obscured and, therefore, taking people far longer to get the help they needed. I wanted people to *see* themselves in the disordered relational patterns of codependency so we could work on the root problems.

I slowly realized that I was looking at codependency from a different vantage point than the old school definition. I saw it through the lens of my client's over-functioning and hypervigilant behaviors and the pain these behaviors were causing. I wasn't attached to any traditional notions. I simply wanted to help them change the behaviors that were causing their exhaustion, burnout, and resentment.

I discovered that a little reframe made a huge difference. I conceived of the term *high-functioning codependency*, or HFC, to describe the flavor of codependency that I was seeing in the majority of my highly capable therapy clients every day. It was also uncannily familiar because it was what I personally experienced for years in my twenties and early thirties. I define HFC as behavior that includes being overly invested in the feeling states, the decisions, the outcomes, and the circumstances of the people in your life to the detriment of your own internal peace and emotional and/or financial well-being. HFC relationships can include blurred boundaries and imbalanced effort and power, with the HFC often taking responsibility for fulfilling the other person's needs and trying to control most aspects of the relationship.

High-functioning codependents are often smart, successful, reliable, and accomplished. They don't identify with being dependent because they are likely doing everything for everyone else. They might have an amazing career, run a household, care for children or aging parents, juggle all the extracurriculars, coordinate the various appointments, and likely life coach their friends through all their problems, too.

Bottom line: the more capable you are, the more codependency doesn't look like codependency. But if you are over-extending, over-functioning, over-giving, and over-focusing on others—and doing way too much—these behaviors are compromising your inner peace and well-being. Regardless of what we call it, it's a problem.

And because we are so damn efficient, we make all our overdoing and over-managing look easy breezy—so no one notices we're suffering.

Loving Reminder 🖤
High-functioning codependency comes at a very high price,
but we don't often realize we are paying it.

To complicate matters further, in our society, many features of HFC-ness (being thoughtful, caring, efficient, generous, selfless) are socially rewarded, making it harder for people to understand how their own behavior is dysfunctional. How often have we heard in childhood, "Be good," or, "Turn that frown upside down," or, "If you don't have something nice to say, don't say anything at all." We are raised and praised to be self-abandoning codependents.

When I added "high-functioning" to the word "codependency" and shared the updated definition, my clients all raised their hand without shame. *It's me. Hi. I'm the problem, it's me.* Suddenly, "codependency" became very relatable. As soon as they self-identified as HFC, my clients experienced a major shift in their self-awareness. Now, we could get to work.

It may be reassuring to know that, in spite of the myths, there is no one type of person who tends to be a high-functioning codependent. We come in all shapes and sizes. Some of us are boisterous and some are more subdued; some funny, others serious; some optimistic, others pragmatic. Some are extroverts and some are introverts. What we have in common are HFC relational behaviors. But *how* we express these behaviors is unique to each person. It's also important to note that many HFCs are often highly sensitive people (HSP) or empaths. They have sensitive nervous systems, are acutely aware of subtle mood shifts in the people around them, and have the potential to feel overwhelmed in highly stimulating environments. When you are an empath, you naturally feel other people's feelings. And, when you're also an HFC, you may feel compelled to help, especially if others' feelings are on the negative side.

Identifying Your HFC Behaviors

To help you recognize where and how HFC may show up in your life, read through the list below of the most common issues that I witness in my therapy clients. Pay attention to what feels relatable to you.

Maybe you identify with a few of these traits or maybe you see yourself in all of them. Either is fine. As you read, avoid beating yourself up for anything you recognize. Identifying what's going on is a courageous first step. You are learning more about yourself and we will use the information for your transformation throughout this book.

- **Communication Challenges**

  You're an expert at knowing the feelings and emotions of the people in your life, but you may be less intimate with your own. This can make effectively communicating your true thoughts and feelings difficult, especially if you fear being rejected, or are conflict avoidant.

- **Approval Seeking**

  You may prioritize other people's needs above your own. Or say yes when you would rather say no, and you likely don't love confrontation. You may apologize often— not only when you're not sorry, but also when you are angry, sad, frustrated, or anxious. You may be afraid of what might happen if you do something that inspires disapproval from someone else, so you subvert your preferences, emotions, and needs.

- **Auto-Fixing**

  When someone is sharing a problem or situation with you, you may immediately jump in and give your opinion of what they should do to fix it whether they asked you or not.

- **Disordered Boundaries**

  When you are outwardly focused on the needs and wants of others, it is difficult to establish and maintain your own healthy boundaries. In addition, you may anticipate others' needs without checking in with them, setting yourself up to overstep their boundaries.

- **Ignoring, Minimizing, or Denying Problems**

  To avoid conflict, you may find yourself saying things like, "I don't want to make a big deal out of nothing," or making excuses for other people's bad behavior such as, "they are just tired and cranky. I know they didn't mean it."

- **Self-Sacrificing**

  Self-sacrifice has long been held up as a virtue in many cultures, but it is important to take a close look at where you are sacrificing what you want and what you need for other people. It could look like not doing things for yourself that would allow you to rest or bring you joy because you are more tuned in to other people's needs than your own.

- **Hyper-Helping**

  You may be in a helping field like nursing, therapy, or coaching where being a natural born helper is a plus. The hyper-helping tendency can easily spill over into your personal life and can look like doing things for others that they can and should do for themselves.

- **Over-Functioning**

  You are often compelled to go way above and beyond for other people, both when they ask for help and when they don't. This tendency can manifest anywhere—at home, at work, in personal and professional relationships, and even with someone you've just met. It's also not sustainable. If you're giving until it hurts, you are more likely to end up feeling bitter or burned-out.

→ CHECK IN

Which of the traits above resonate with you? If it was every single one, don't worry. You are exactly where you need to be. If it was just a few, that's great, too. You are learning more about who you truly are. Remember: this is a no-judgment zone.

At their core, codependent relationships are built on a foundation of disordered boundaries and dysfunctional relational patterns with a covert or overt bid for control of *someone else's* situation. That last part might be hard to understand and accept. It definitely was for me.

In my life, pre-HFC recovery, I was not consciously trying to control anything. But I was actively trying to stop conflict and drama before they began. Like other HFCs, my drive to control situations and people was rooted in fear. Fear of the unknown. Fear of what terrible thing would happen if I didn't intercede. Fear of having a situation spin out of control. Fear of others being angry, upset, or unhappy.

As loving, caring people, all of us are invested in the happiness of those we care about. But high-functioning codependents are *overly* invested. One HFC I met at a conference said plainly, "I have a tendency to scan every room and situation for impending issues. It's like my problem meter has no off setting. I just want people to be happy. If I'm honest, it can be *exhausting*." Constantly being afraid and needing to be in control *is* exhausting.

The Mask of Highly Capable People

The tricky thing about HFCs is that they are so competent, they can effectively mask their disordered behavior. Few in their circles can actually see that they're tired, suffering, and sometimes seething. That's because the HFC is busy being on top of things:

sending flowers for birthdays, remembering important anniversary dates, showing up to help when Grandma's furniture needs to be lugged away, going the extra mile for the big presentation—and more. In fact, most people around HFCs think they're doing *great*. They don't see the crack in the veneer or know what's happening inside.

And that is the HFC way—to consistently present a polished package of efficiency.

I'm fine.

No need to worry about me.

It's all good.

I got it.

Sometimes, HFCs' masks are so good, they can't even recognize their own over-functioning tendencies.

Pre-recovery, most HFCs are unaware that in all their tasking, checking things off lists, and endless doing for others, they've made an unconscious and consequential choice—to neglect the most foundational relationship of all, the one that they have with themselves.

Loving Reminder 🖤

As you are raising your self-awareness, remember that this is a process. It's going to take some time and repetition to create healthier relational patterns—and you can do it.

Over-Functioning

Let's expand on one of the most significant issues for HFCs: over-functioning. For Andrea, it seemed that neglecting and overriding her own needs, coupled with the chronic stress of her over-functioning, led to the panic attack. It was a physical cue that she was doing *too much*.

In our sessions, I explained high-functioning codependency, illustrating the concept by pointing out her numerous over-functioning, over-giving, and over-extending behaviors—from offering to help her neighbor's son with his college essay, right down to bringing an extra toiletry kit to her friend for her wedding night ("just in case she forgot the toothpaste"). Andrea nodded in recognition and said, "Okay, I can see that."

To begin the process of change, the first step was to raise her self-awareness about her behaviors, choices, and reactions.

In our next session, we explored why she always felt like she was The One to make life happen for herself and others. "Oh, that's easy. If I don't do it, no one will," she said.

This is a common belief and one of the biggest mental hurdles to overcome—how we may feel that we *have* to be the one to do all the things, all the time, whether someone asks us to or not.

Like most HFCs, Andrea's get-it-done behaviors were often genuinely helpful. After all, there were certain things that just came easily to her, like planning which rest stop to go to on the way to her husband's family's house. Or which cafe had the best breakfast sandwiches for the road. Or how to navigate tricky office or social politics without causing a time-sucking drama.

Not only was she a superstar in every sense, but she'd also gotten used to being praised for her efficiency and thoughtfulness. Everyone wanted, even expected, that level of service and consideration from her. What *she* genuinely wanted was the only question that really mattered, but being so outwardly focused, it was the question she rarely considered. Her self-reflection was the beginning of new awareness, which is where all transformation begins.

BACK TO YOU
How Can You Tell If You're Overly Invested?

Imagine your partner, friend, or sibling coming to you in a crisis.

☐ How urgent does their situation feel to you?

☐ Does it immediately feel like *your* problem to fix?

☐ What's your first instinctive reaction?

For most HFCs, a call like this will send them straight into a fix-it tailspin. Depending on the crisis, they're Googling house cleaning services, scheduling the food delivery, and researching divorce lawyers—with little regard to whatever they were doing before.

If some version of that happens for you—believing it's your job to manage your partner/friend/sibling's situation, and do it immediately—I see you, pal. This is a codependent response.

Resentment

Not surprisingly, this over-functioning way of life creates an undercurrent of resentment, which, naturally, is going to bubble to the surface from time to time. (Remember Andrea's favorite refrain? "Why is everyone so inefficient?") Some HFCs will feel upset when their loved ones *don't* heed their well-meaning guidance and heroic gestures of support. If you find yourself feeling chronically annoyed, perturbed, and maybe even downright bitter, consider that you may be doing *too much*.

It's also possible that you are suppressing your resentment with rationalizations. As HFCs, we easily chalk up our over-investment in the lives of our loved ones to our care and concern for their well-being—and sometimes for the well-being of all of humanity. For example, you notice that an acquaintance you follow online just posted about losing her son in a car accident. Suddenly you feel like you *must* get her the name of an excellent grief counselor, or, at the very least, rally her friends to get a meal train going. (Like I said, HFCs are often codependent with the world at large.) But this type of over-investment borders on intrusive. It is also not sustainable. We're mere mortals, just like everyone else, with needs, dreams, and responsibilities that require our care and attention. This can be news for HFCs.

> ### Say It with Me 💬
> My worth and value are determined by who I am,
> not how much I do for others.

People-pleasing

The fact is, if we are over-functioning and overly focused on the feeling states and life situations of others, our authentic feelings may be buried beneath the rubble of tasking, doing, and managing. People-pleasing can be a catalyst for these behaviors. As author and podcast host Glennon Doyle says, "When a woman finally learns that pleasing the world is impossible, she becomes free to learn how to please herself." Amen, sister.

There are many reasons we become people pleasers. Maybe we were taught to be "good" and that meant going along with what others wanted, regardless of our wants, needs, and desires. We tend to hide our real feelings instead of rocking the boat with our authenticity. Often, people pleasers start off as parent pleasers raised in households where not pleasing a parent could have stressful or even dangerous consequences. And a lot of us are simply wired this way, driven by a primal fear of being kicked out of the pack. We want to make sure others are okay so that *we* can be okay, too.

With people-pleasing, we tend to have anxiety and fear around being judged, not being liked, and letting others down. We attempt to influence other people's feeling states and experiences to avoid these fates—and that is the core of people-pleasing. *I want you to approve of me, so I will alter my behavior to get that approval. I want you to like me even if I don't particularly like you.* (Which makes no logical sense but is super common.)

People pleasers want to be seen as "nice," but in truth, saying yes when you want to say no is not only *not* nice, it's misleading. You are basically giving faulty information about who you are and where you stand. This is especially important in your intimate relationships because how can anyone authentically love you if they don't authentically know you? The truth is, they can't.

Ultimately, you will most likely end up pleasing others in ways that are not so pleasing to yourself. That's an unavoidable fact.

Tolerating Too Much

As HFCs, we are accustomed to a constant outflow of energy— picking up the slack, scanning situations and people to make sure that everything (and everyone) is okay, handling whatever needs to be handled. In that process, we don't even realize what we might be tolerating.

We tend to accept, take on, put up with, and be negatively impacted by other people's bad behavior, unmet needs, boundary violations, incompleteness, issues, resentments, and even our own self-sabotaging behavior. As capable as you are, trying to avoid potential drama can keep you tolerating more than you should.

Raising awareness in this area will eventually become the GPS to show you the way to a healthier style of relating to others, as well as yourself.

The following are big and small real-life examples from my community of what people tolerate:

- Nonstop complaints from immediate family

- Fake friends and chronic interrupters

- Always being the one to travel to see family

- Poor treatment / silent treatment / gaslighting and other abusive behavior

- Disrespect from kids or stepkids

- Bearing the brunt of hostility under the guise of a "joke"

- Double standards in relationships; for example, the friend who takes her sweet time in replying (if at all) but expects an insta-response when she's the one reaching out

- Doing more than your share of the housework

- Self-sabotage and self-medicating with alcohol

- Comments about weight and appearance

- Regularly being on the receiving end of other people's drama and stress

Some of these experiences might last for just a moment, but if we ignore how we really feel, the impact stays with us for much longer. We may ruminate or be irritated without knowing the source. It's exhausting.

→ CHECK IN

You are likely tolerating more than you may realize. Take a couple of minutes to list in your journal ten situations, circumstances, people, or feelings that you are tolerating right now.

We Can Change—and It's Worth It

HFCs carry a whole stadium of data about other people in their heads—who likes what kind of cheese or wine, who has an aversion to air conditioning, who can't stand small talk, and so on. Yet, while we're so mindful of what other people's likes and dislikes are, we rarely extend that same level of courtesy and thought to ourselves.

> *Loving Reminder* 🖤
> You deserve more than what you're tolerating.

Like Andrea, you and every HFC I've ever encountered, are humans with exceptionally bright lights and a vast capacity to care about others. In many ways, you're the masters of the universe. You are managing a lot in life and that takes a certain amount of confidence, decision-making ability, and action. Andrea was starting to discover just how adaptable and resilient she was. After her panic attack, she even began to view the event as a blessing in disguise—a way to reclaim her bandwidth and her life. She was now intentionally on a journey of self-discovery and committed to creating a better, healthier way of relating. Recovery, for Andrea and all of us, is about stopping the high-cost behaviors of HFC to create the space to know, develop, and celebrate our innate selves.

Armed with strength and courage, the process of real-deal change is also bolstered when you align yourself with healthier habits and behaviors *gradually*—by learning to identify what is (and is not) your responsibility. Slowly but surely, you can learn to do this.

It may feel daunting to even think about changing these deeply ingrained behavioral patterns but trust me (and science): you *can* teach your old brain new tricks. We now know that the brain's neural connections—estimated to be in the ballpark of a whopping one hundred trillion—are formed and potentially altered anew every single day, thanks to our lived experiences. This is called neuroplasticity. If we continue engaging in our disordered but familiar habits and patterns, we're reinforcing the old neural pathways and staying stuck. Yet with concerted, consistent effort, we can create new neural pathways and healthier relational patterns, increasing our well-being exponentially.

As you go through the rest of these pages, remember that your skills and gifts are unique. No one else can do this work for you. These are your life lessons to learn and it's a privilege to do so.

There's more happiness, freedom, and satisfaction on the other side. Your most important responsibility is the one you have to yourself—to nurture your own unique energies, talents, and passions. Leaving behind your reflex to do *too much* opens the door to abundant energy, bandwidth, and joy, providing the fuel you need to thrive in all areas of your life.

▶ TAKE ACTION ◀

- **Top of Mind.** Pay attention to how often you compromise your own needs. Over the next forty-eight hours, observe each time you: (1) Say yes when you really want to say no; (2) apologize, especially if you're not sorry, or when you're actually feeling angry; or (3) avoid confrontation or put someone else's needs above your own.

- **Take Care.** As soon as you realize you're over-functioning (you're on someone else's side of the street) stop and count to twenty. Then, turn your attention back to yourself.

- **Go Deeper: Codependent Relationship Questionnaire.** The more you know about yourself, the easier it will be to shift how you interact in your relationships. Go to page 229 in the "Go Deeper" section at the back of the book to uncover your relationship patterns.

CHAPTER 2

Caring vs. Codependent

BY MY EARLY THIRTIES, I had become pretty skilled at "doing life." Running the New York office of a bicoastal talent agency, brokering high-value deals, and earning the respect of my peers—*check*. Going to grad school to become a therapist and creating a career that aligned with my values—*check*. Surrounded by awesome, inspiring, drama-free friends—*check*. Getting high on life (sober) for close to a decade and deeply invested in my own therapeutic life and personal evolution—*check*. In a passionate, healthy, and reciprocal relationship with a man I deeply loved and building our family with his three teenage boys—*check*.

For the first time ever, I felt peace and freedom within. My life was both full and wonderful, and I somehow managed to keep all the various balls in the air—that is, until my older sister Jenna found herself in crisis. Then, all my Zen went flying out the window.

Jenna had a history of substance abuse and bad romances, but her latest rough patch was "code red" territory. Ever since she moved in with her abusive, drug addicted a-hole of a boyfriend, she'd been blowing up my phone with SOS calls, eager to relay every detail of his drunken tirades. Their fights had even turned physical. Making matters a million times worse, my beloved sister was completely isolated, living with a jerk in a shack in the woods that had no electricity or running water. You can understand why my blood pressure spiked every time she called. It didn't matter where I was—at the office, about to sit down for dinner, wrangling the boys to do their homework, in bed seconds away from blissful shut-eye—the moment I'd see her name on pop up, my chest would clench, and it felt like I had no oxygen supply. *What now?* I'd think.

The truth is, I didn't want to admit my worst fear, that one of these days, the phone call would reach the level of full-blown catastrophe, and I'd lose Jenna forever. In these fearful moments, all that mattered was getting her to safety. I lost sight of my own blessings.

In time, I started to notice a pattern. She'd call with another painfully true horror story ("he pushed me, he threw me out in a snowstorm, he claimed I flirted with a guy at the liquor store"), and I'd listen, filled with dread and determination. "Let's figure this out," I'd say, offering up every single remedy I could think of. "I have a book on escaping abusive relationships that I've underlined for you and will arrive in your mailbox tomorrow. I found a great therapist for you. I talked to a lawyer who specializes in domestic violence." I begged her to leave him and temporarily move in with me and my then-boyfriend-now-husband, Victor, (who I refer to by his nickname "Vic" throughout the rest of the book) and the kids. "Please, Jenna—we have room. You can get sober and into therapy, and life will be *so* much better." The fix was so simple, according to me. All she had to do was consent.

Every time, she'd thank me for my support and advice, saying, "God, I feel so much better just talking to you. Thank you!" I, on the other hand, did not feel better after our calls. I felt awful. The black cloud of Jenna's toxic environment transferred into my body, making me want to vomit. My emotional hangover would last two solid days. Have you ever heard the saying, "Alcoholics don't have relationships, they take hostages"? Well, if you've ever loved one, you know how true that statement is. With Jenna and this impossibly bad situation, I definitely felt like I'd been taken hostage.

When A-hole's derogatory comments and the injustice of it all started to play in my mind, I defaulted to fantasy action-mode—*Do I call the cops and rat him out for having drugs? Or get my cousin Mikey to kick the crap out of him?*

Soon, it felt like I rarely thought about anything else. With my besties as well as with Vic and the boys, I was often distracted, ruminating obsessively about Jenna in my determination to liberate her from hell. I was sometimes so fixed in worry that I might as well have been on a different planet.

Then one day, I hung up with Jenna and felt sadness wash over me. Before I knew it, I was leaning with my back against the refrigerator, sobbing as I slid down to the floor. *How could my beautiful, funny, strong sister be caught up with such a monster? Why couldn't she just accept my help?* For the first time, I allowed myself to fully experience the profound sadness and grief over this impossible situation. Vic walked in and sat beside me as I cried on the floor.

"Oh, Ter," he said. "Jenna?"

Still crying, I nodded yes and thought, *Something has to change.*

At my next session with Bev, my badass, truth-telling therapist, I was still very tender and teary, but when I started to speak, frustration, fear, and fury came out. "Bev, I've done everything I can think of to help Jenna get out and get help! I've sent her money, offered ten thousand escape plans, but she's not doing *anything*. What am I going to do?"

I hoped Bev would reply with *the* answer of how I could fix Jenna's problems, but instead, she took a long pause. Looking at me with great compassion, she asked, "What makes you think that you know what lessons your sister needs to learn in this lifetime?"

Initially, I rejected the entire premise of Bev's question. Obviously, anyone with an ounce of common sense could see that my sister didn't need to learn any lessons by being abused by a drug-addicted POS. "She could learn those lessons while safe with us, hundreds of miles away from this a-hole, in a home with a functional water tank. I think we can all agree on that!" I exclaimed defensively.

Bev looked me in the eye and said calmly, "Actually, Terri, I can't agree with that. I don't know what your sister needs to learn. I'm not God."

My interpretation of Bev's comment was that it's impossible for us to know what is right for another person—when we don't live in their hearts—and it's self-important and egotistical to presume that we do. This *I-know-exactly-what-you-should-be-doing* belief can be harmful to our own mental well-being, too, as I was slowly learning.

Bev reminded me of how hard I'd worked over the last decade to build a beautiful, harmonious, and functional life for myself. My sister's dumpster fire of a situation—or, more precisely, the fact that she would not leave that blazing mess—was threatening my hard-won peace.

"What you really want is for Jenna to get it together, so that *your* pain can end," Bev explained.

Wow, I thought. Her wisdom hit me like a freight train of truth. *You are not wrong.*

I was so obsessed with controlling the outcome of my sister's life that I was neglecting my own emotional needs, my own family, and my own well-being. *Yikes.*

This mind-blowing reframe immediately brought my self-image into question. I truly believed that my care and concern for Jenna (and the rest of the world) was born out of selfless, Mother Teresa-style love. I mean, I didn't *actually* think I was Mother Teresa, but as a kind and empathic person, I really thought I was doing right by Jenna, by everyone. It had never even entered my mind that my need for Jenna to get the hell out of Dodge was motivated, at least in part, by my desire for my own pain to end. I tried to wrap my head around this distressing and humbling truth: my need to free her was more about me than I'd realized.

As HFCs, we are driven by a desire for peace because we are always *on*, always planning, plotting, and doing. Somewhere along the way, we unconsciously take responsibility for other people's feelings *and lives,* to the detriment of our own well-being. That's exactly what I'd done with Jenna.

Until this game-changer of a revelation with Bev, I had no clue that what I thought was straight up caring was actually soaked in codependency. For any HFC, it is hugely helpful to understand the difference, so let's parse these subtle but powerful distinctions.

Caring . . . or Codependent?

Many HFCs are the lovers, the caregivers, the healers, the resident "moms" and "therapists" wherever we go (work, home, the co-op, and so on). If you are identifying as an HFC, it's a safe bet that your heart is in the right place, like mine was with Jenna. So, it can be challenging to accept that—despite the best intentions—our codependent actions may be misguided.

Whenever I explore the "codependent versus caring" distinction with clients and students, I inevitably hear, "What's wrong with being nice?" The answer is—nothing at all. In fact, *helper's high* is a legit phenomenon that describes the increased feelings of fulfillment and well-being that arise from lending someone else a hand.

It feels great to give money to your BFF's daughter who is running a charity race, or to sign up to make a home-cooked meal for a loved one recovering from a health crisis. Truly healthy, loving, and appropriate giving can create feel-good vibes all around. However, if you are chronically giving, doing, and over-functioning from a place of fear in order to dictate outcomes, feel valued, recognized, or even loved, that's more dysfunctional and codependent than genuine caring.

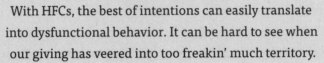

Loving Reminder 🖤

With HFCs, the best of intentions can easily translate
into dysfunctional behavior. It can be hard to see when
our giving has veered into too freakin' much territory.

Unhealthy Helping

So much of the time, we can see our helping as just being "nice," but the truth is that there is a tipping point where our compulsion to jump into someone else's situation may be less about their needs and more about our own.

The concept of *unhealthy helping*—"helpful" behaviors that are unintentionally *unhelpful*—was originated by Shawn Meghan Burn, PhD, a psychologist, researcher, and the author of *Unhealthy Helping: A Psychological Guide to Overcoming Codependence, Enabling, and Other Dysfunctional Giving.* In exploring the unintended consequences of dysfunctional giving, Burn writes, "Some types of helping and giving create unhealthy dependencies and reduce others' self-confidence, competency, and life skills." So, when we engage in unhealthy helping, we are making others dependent on us and sending the disempowering message that they don't have what it takes to handle their own business.

Consider the following: if you are a parent who is always sending your adult kid cash to cover their monthly rent, your support may be solving their cash flow problem in the short-term, but you're contributing to a longer-term problem by preventing them from facing the consequences of their poor money management. Without feeling the squeeze of being overdrawn or having to buck up and ask their landlord for an extension, your child loses motivation to create their own fiscal security. Over time, taking responsibility for a situation that is not, in fact, your responsibility will chip away at *their* self-confidence and self-esteem.

Why do we engage in unhealthy helping behaviors? A lot of my clients over the years have said things like, "I see myself as a helpful person—it's just who I am," or, "I like to be needed." Here's the thing: If we are *pushing* our help on someone else, then is it really about them? Or are we doing what *we* need to feel valuable or okay?

Other people have a right to make mistakes, to fail, to flail, to not be doing the things we think they should be doing. To paraphrase Bev, none of us are God.

BACK TO YOU
When Is Your Helping Unhealthy?

If you are wondering if your way of showing kindness, generosity, and care is really genuine, or if your version of "helping" tips into codependency, ask yourself the following questions:

- ☐ Am I helping because I want to, or do I feel obligated?

- ☐ Do I spend a lot of time worrying about someone else's problems?

- ☐ Do I feel anxious, purposeless, or empty when I'm not helping someone?

- ☐ Do I give unasked-for advice?

- ☐ Do I give or help in ways that negatively affect my well-being and sense of self?

- ☐ Are my relationships out of balance because I give but find it hard to receive?

- ☐ Do I encourage independence or dependence through my helping?

□ Am I enabling or helping?

Use your answers to identify where unhealthy helping (codependency) is at play in your relationships. The more you understand your unique style of relating the easier it will be to know where to focus your time and attention. Remember, self-knowledge is the foundation for your healing and recovery.

Compulsive Reactions

So often, as HFCs, we give and help without pausing to consider if we *actually* want to be giving or helping in the ways we feel instantly compelled to. We may simply hook our focus on what's going to help avoid conflict. We are motivated by what we think is best for others, and what's going to cause us the least amount of short-term stress.

A few years back, I went to get my hair done at my fave salon in New York City on a busy Saturday. After applying a thirty-minute hair mask, an assistant set me up in a seat at one of the sinks while I waited. Antennas up, I couldn't help but notice that there were a lot of folks waiting for a sink. The longer the sink line got, the more anxious I became. *Was the sweet assistant going to get into trouble? Was someone going to complain to the manager? Were the people wait-ing judging me as selfish for taking up a sink when I could have waited elsewhere?* These were the thoughts swirling around in my mind, so I flagged the assistant and asked, "Want me to move so you can have this sink?" She smiled. "No, you're good."

On the surface, this seemed like a normal exchange—I was being considerate, right? The assistant might have even viewed my gesture as thoughtful. Yet having been an HFC in recovery for almost two decades at this point, I knew that this kind of psycho-logical machination is never without cause—or cost.

Besides auto-accomodating (what I did at the salon), another common unconscious HFC behavior is anticipatory planning. In both cases, you may naturally slip into these behaviors almost without noticing.

Auto-accommodating. Auto-accommodating is a state of hyper-awareness, where you are acutely dialed into what is happening around you, unconsciously scanning for ways to ward off conflict or correct problems, even if said conflict or problems have nothing whatsoever to do with you. It is always being ready to lessen someone's burden or to help, even without being asked. It is an unconscious mechanism, so you may not realize how responsible you're feeling for everything and everyone around you.

Even when we've been in solid recovery from HFC for years, auto-accommodating is one of those deeply ingrained habits that can crop up out of nowhere and drain us of precious energy. Have you ever discovered that your laptop was running slowly because you had a large file or program sucking up its bandwidth? Well, being an auto-accommodator is like that. Our mind-body-spirit system is drained by automatic, compulsive, and unconscious programming that has us overly dialed into our environments, perpetually in a state of hyper-sensory sensitivity.

Whatever form it takes, acting from unconscious reactions is not acting freely—it's *reacting* to whatever might be causing us angst in our environment. Resisting this type of reaction is *vital* to stopping HFC behaviors in their tracks. When the urge to spring into action is so strong we can't *not* do it, that's a telltale sign that we're compulsively reacting and not acting from choice.

In the case of the hair salon, those were professionals running one of the busiest salons in Manhattan. What made me think that I, Terri Cole, had the best plan for managing their customer flow? This was so not my side of the street.

Afterwards, I thought, *How might I have otherwise spent my time if I weren't assuming responsibility for something that wasn't mine?* I could have taken those moments to meditate, or listen to music, or enjoy just resting my brain. Truth is, I'll never know how I might have spent that precious time. When we talk about the cost of doing business as an HFC, this is what we mean: that time and energy we've spent worrying about other people's side of the street is now and forever gone. And we can't get our time back. What you are learning in this book is raising your awareness so that you can consciously choose less depleting behaviors in the future.

→ CHECK IN

Is the term auto-accommodator *new to you? Think about an instance where you reflexively jumped in to fix a situation that was not yours to fix. If you stop and think for a moment, can you identify what thoughts or feelings motivated your actions?*

Anticipatory Planning. Another compulsive and draining behavior is anticipatory planning, or trying to prevent anyone from getting upset by arranging situations *just so*, ahead of time, leaving no detail untouched.

Years ago, I was planning a couples road trip and one of my girlfriends was in a relationship with a challenging personality. I found myself ruminating over all the ways I could preemptively avoid conflict with this person who had a history of ruining our gatherings with their drama. How could I make them more comfortable and meet all their needs so they wouldn't instigate problems or torture my friend? That is called *codependent anticipation*. It encompasses the anxiety (and fix-it behaviors) that precedes a situation where there *might* be conflict.

When we're engaged in anticipatory planning, we're spending way too much time worrying in advance and taking Herculean steps—over-planning, over-doing, and over-functioning—to avoid potential upset or conflict. For instance, when you check in with your dinner guests about food restrictions, that's considerate. But if your mind loops on stress-fueled thoughts of how guests might feel, behave, or interact with each other, that's anticipatory planning. It's similar to auto-accommodating in that you're in a state of hyper-awareness, but different in that it happens before you enter an environment.

> ### Say It with Me 💬
> I am happy and grateful to be establishing
> healthier connections and relationships.

Fear

As we established in chapter 1, when in problem-solving, auto-fixing mode, our actions as HFCs are often fear-based, driven by an unconscious need to control the outcomes, feeling states, and experiences of others. It's a need that can be so forceful, it springs us into all kinds of action that would be truly impressive if it weren't making us hyper-focused on changing, fixing, and saving others, regularly bypassing our own needs.

Looking back, it's kind of remarkable how much energy I was putting toward my sister Jenna's situation when I also had a full-time job, a new-ish relationship, and three stepkids who definitely needed my time and attention. But my compulsive behavior came from the sheer terror that something *more* terrible might happen to my sister. In my mind, "hands off the wheel" was not an option because her situation made me feel so powerless and that feeling was intolerable. Then Bev began to open my eyes to what was really going on in my Mission Impossible quest (no, really) to save Jenna. My actions were more a desperate bid for control than a healthy expression of my free will to help. But it was also so darn sneaky I couldn't even see it.

Yet as my breaking point in the kitchen demonstrated, there's only so long a person can be driven by compulsion and *not* face the consequences to her own bandwidth and well-being. Over the years, I've treated and encountered many women at the end of their rope, experiencing exhaustion and other physical conditions, like auto-immune disorders, TMJ, irritable bowel syndrome, and burnout. Having been there, I understood their fatigue firsthand. Of course they were super tired—just like anyone would be who constantly back-burners their own self-care and is always last on their own list. Nearly all were blind to their compulsive behaviors and sought help to address either their stress-related physical symptoms or a loved one's dire pain. It often took time for them to gain awareness around their emotional pain. For most of us, we're way more comfortable keeping our focus on other people's stuff than acknowledging our own. And when self-sacrificing and self-abandonment are our default settings—well, speaking from experience—the impending implosion is just a matter of time.

It can be helpful to see how acting from compulsion or fear can lead to controlling behaviors, including auto–advice giving, which inevitably leads us to inserting ourselves and interfering with others' situations. As with most HFC behaviors, you may not even be aware that you're engaging in them.

Auto–advice Giving. The moment someone in your orbit—relative, pal, colleague, random flight attendant—so much as hints at a problem, do you find yourself naturally turning your mental dial to the "fix it" channel and offering grade-A, but unsolicited, advice? This behavior is what I call *auto–advice giving*, a common HFC move to be helpful (consciously) and manage our own discomfort (unconsciously). To avoid our unease with someone else's discomfort, we whip out strategies, doctor referrals, sage bits of research-backed advice, and relevant personal anecdotes. Our well of sound solutions runs deep.

When we do this, we are inadvertently centering *ourselves* in whatever situation others are grappling with, when the reality is we can't actually know what they should do. Even if our heart is in the right place, it's *their* situation, not ours.

Let's consider the following hypothetical example: a colleague confides in you because she's just had a fight with her partner over their future. He wants kids, she doesn't. Instead of listening to her with an open, compassionate ear, you mentally gather your ideas, thoughts, and judgments about what's right for her. As she's about to dissolve into tears, you come up with a plan, "Here's the name of a great couple's therapist. Grab a copy of *The Baby Decision* because you might just want to rethink the no kids thing—just to cover all your bases."

We may not realize it, but when we're automatically citing from *the-world-according-to-me*, we're missing out on some of the richest parts of human interaction, which is the give and take of sharing and listening. In this example, you are seeing your colleague through a reactionary, *must help* lens tinged with your own desires and life experiences. Your colleague is not recognized for her strength or who she might become as a result of her struggle. And you've defaulted to a familiar utilitarian role where your value is only as good as what you can do for others. The real connection can get lost in that stream of excellent advice.

Complicating matters, some folks welcome our interference. Jenna, for example, kept calling me for advice and support. She clearly wasn't offended by me inserting myself into her crisis, but even in the cases where our problem-solving is gladly received, there are still unintended consequences to our interference. Not only are we exhausted, but we're also losing out on the opportunity to truly be present with our loved ones (or any human being) and allow them to figure things out. This chronic imposition is a surefire way to diminish the substantial value of human-to-human connection. So much is lost.

To be clear, this doesn't mean you should never ever again share your thoughts or opinions with the folks in your life. It means you can learn to do so mindfully and with respect to the other person's autonomy. (More on this in chapter 10.)

BACK TO YOU
Insert a Power Pause

In your next conversation, observe how you relate and respond to the other person. When do you feel compelled to jump in? How do you handle natural silences? What dynamic makes you the most uncomfortable? (Also notice when you feel the most *comfortable*—is it when you're doing the talking or advice-giving?). This is all food for thought.

A power pause in a conversation may provide a moment to think, inspire someone to share themselves more deeply with you, or allow a conversation to go in a different direction. It can be an opportunity to observe and go with the flow.

When most HFCs start to look under the hood and see that their behaviors are not always motivated only by lovingkindness, it can feel mortifying. But as an HFC in recovery, I can sincerely say that it's better to raise your self-awareness and risk this (temporary) discomfort than to stay in a pattern of behaviors and relating that is stealing your precious peace, time, and well-being. You don't have to be perfect; you just have to be willing to unlearn the disordered behavioral patterns that are not optimal for the life you deserve.

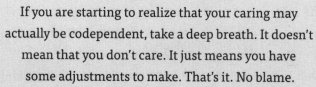

> *Loving Reminder* 🖤
> If you are starting to realize that your caring may
> actually be codependent, take a deep breath. It doesn't
> mean that you don't care. It just means you have
> some adjustments to make. That's it. No blame.

Other Catalysts of HFC Behavior

When Bev helped me see my behaviors with Jenna as codependent instead of one hundred percent caring, I started thinking about all of my behaviors and reactions in a completely different way. It was uncomfortable, but I was motivated by my trust in Bev. By that time, we had been working together for years, and so I placed great value in her wisdom. She was a skilled clinician, and her sage observations propelled me forward when I felt completely lost in the woods. Without that trust, I don't know how much longer it would have taken me to step outside the endless loop of unconscious and compulsive behavior.

With her guidance, I started reflecting hard. And one thing became clear: *I truly believed that I had to be the one to solve Jenna's situation.* The question was, *Why?*

The answer to that question was complicated. For HFCs, a combination of guiding beliefs, qualities, experiences, and behaviors keep informing our behavior. My behavior with Jenna was fueled by fear, guilt, and a desire to control that tipped the scale toward codependency and away from healthy caring. Recognizing and reflecting on the factors that drive your behavior is integral to your transformation.

"It Has to Be Me"

This is one of the most common refrains of HFCs. Whether we're admitting this to ourselves or not, the compulsion in our behavior is reflective of the belief that if *we* don't handle shit, no one will. This was definitely true for me in the Jenna situation.

Perhaps you have seen this mindset played out in different parts of your life. *If I don't provide a solid strategy for my coworker, they will fail.* Or, *if I don't bail my niece out of jail, her life trajectory is screwed.* Or, *if I don't show up at the hospital to take care of my sick friend, he will receive subpar care and feel terribly alone.*

In my case, I genuinely felt that if I didn't single-handedly wrangle Jenna from her mess, no one would. The worst-case scenarios running in my head were enough to keep me on this treadmill.

No question, my designated role as family hero was in full effect as I tried to "save" Jenna from her own choices.

Complicating matters, I was driven by a sense of profound fear, not only of what might happen to Jenna (painfully conscious), but of what might happen to *me* if I were not the one in charge (painfully unconscious). Was I failing her? Was I a bad sister? Would I be judged or rejected by my family if I failed to fix her situation? Acting out of fear means that we are not coming from a place of conscious choices.

My attempt to save Jenna gave me a false sense of security—at least I was doing *something*. At least she had me to count on. At the very least, if I didn't give up, there was still hope.

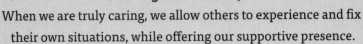

Loving Reminder 💚
When we are truly caring, we allow others to experience and fix their own situations, while offering our supportive presence.

Guilt

Aside from my overwhelming fear and my need to try to manage an out-of-control situation, there was also the guilt I felt. Guilt is another common HFC driver, and there are many reasons we may feel guilty. One of the most common is becoming more successful than others in your family. Many HFCs are cycle breakers, whether it's avoiding toxic relationships or abstaining from substance abuse, or something else. When it came to Jenna, because she was unhappy and hurting, I felt guilt for being happy and successful, for finding Vic and the boys, and for not being able to help her more. It is not uncommon for HFCs to carry guilt specifically around their loyalty to their family of origin, whether or not they have created a family of their own. We try to be all the things for all the people, and it's just not feasible. But acting out of guilt doesn't make our relationships better. It just makes our lives more stressful and less satisfying.

For many, our compulsive and unconscious actions are a means of securing love and validation. We receive a sense of personal value by being the best fixer, advice-giver, problem-solver, auto-accommodator, and all-around self-assigned hero. We secure a sense of belonging by adding value to others, while often ignoring our own needs in the process. Deep down, we might be taking actions with the unconscious desire to become irreplaceable and essential to others, which can feel like a way to protect ourselves from being rejected.

When our utility to others determines our value, we struggle with feeling good enough. If for some reason we can't provide value to others, we risk having to confront how we feel about ourselves.

With my sister, Jenna, my unconscious choices became untenable. I could not control her behavior, but with Bev's help, I was able to clearly distinguish what my choices and responsibilities were. That was the start of unlearning these self-abandoning, over-functioning, HFC behaviors, and asserting authority over my own experiences.

Jenna had to find the right next move on her own timeline, *and* it was unhealthy and unhelpful for me to make myself constantly available to listen to stories that made me so very anxious and unsettled. Bev helped me to understand that it wasn't that I *shouldn't* save my sister, it's that I *couldn't*. Because it was not possible. But I could and should protect myself. What a monumental relief it was to be let off the hook.

As an HFC in recovery, I can promise you that the moment you realize that you are truly not responsible for others in the way that you might be imagining, you will have one of the most liberating experiences of your life. It's freeing, expanding, and humbling, all at the same time. Once the lightbulb went on for me with Jenna, I started to reflect on my overall style of relating. That's where the humbling part came in. I thought, *Wow, she is not the only person I relate to like this.* That was huge for my healing and the recovery of my bandwidth and internal peace.

Loving Reminder
You're unlearning some deeply ingrained
behavioral patterns, so be gentle and generous with
yourself. Rome wasn't built in a day.

At this stage of the game, treat yourself gently. As scary as this might feel at times, you are still in control of this process and, most importantly, yourself. Right now, focus less on outside-world action and more on reconfiguring internal beliefs and drivers. Sustainable transformation happens from the inside out.

▶ TAKE ACTION ◀

- **Top of Mind.** Take the next twenty-four hours to notice every time you jump in—or think about jumping in—to "fix" in a situation that is not your own. This will give you a clearer idea of what situations kick up your need to auto-accommodate, auto-plan, or automatically give advice so you can choose a different action and save your bandwidth for something else.

- **Take Care.** Embrace moments of stillness and allow yourself to simply be. If the idea of doing nothing feels daunting, grab a journal and explore your feelings about stillness. What makes it uncomfortable? How does it feel to just pause?

- **Go Deeper: Caring or Codependent Exercise.** To make mindful choices in our relationships, we need to understand the difference between caring and codependent behaviors. Go to page 233 in the "Go Deeper" section at the back of the book and do the Caring or Codependent exercise to help you learn healthier ways of relating.

CHAPTER 3

Your HFC Blueprint

Why You Relate the Way You Do

ADA, A SUCCESSFUL beauty influencer, had initially come to see me because she was struggling in a new romantic relationship. In our first session, she got down to brass tacks: "I cannot navigate this man alone."

"That's a strong statement," I replied. "Tell me about your relationship."

Her boyfriend, John, had been a loyal friend for several months as she established herself in a new city, hundreds of miles away from where she grew up. John treated her far better than the string of noncommittal men she was casually dating. When she was upset, John felt her pain. When she was happy, he shared in her joy. Once she realized that she felt more seen by him than she'd ever been, even by her ex-partners, she figured, *I should give this good man a shot.* Yet a week after they became pals-turned-lovers, she found herself in totally unfamiliar territory. One afternoon, she asked him what he was up to. His response rocked her. *Wow,* he texted back, *I didn't peg you for being so insecure and controlling.* Stunned, she had to check that she was actually texting with John. *Was this even the same man?*

The punishment clearly did not fit the "crime." Moments later, John, recognizing the error of his ways, FaceTimed her with a grand apology. Teary, he explained, "No woman has ever been kind to me or even there for me. You are so genuine and amazing. I don't deserve your goodness and love."

His pain melted Ada's heart. She'd been through a bad romance or two in her life. She immediately forgave his volcanic eruption, and they went back to Love Land, or at least, she tried to go back.

One month later, she was already at her wit's end. She explained that she was dealing with erratic, hot and cold behavior from him. He'd been amazing before when they were just friends. She kept thinking if she returned his loyalty and reassured him, he'd settle into the relationship. Ada could not settle at all until her partner was happy. As I got to know her, I saw the pattern of her own happiness being dependent on the other person's.

In true HFC fashion, no one would have guessed she was struggling in her relationship. Online, her life looked perfect. She had a huge, dedicated fanbase, and this success translated to a robust travel schedule and lucrative brand partnerships. Because she made exponentially more than her two siblings, Ada quietly supported them through their times of need, helping cover essentials (rent, medical bills, winter coats) as well as nonessentials, like concerts and trips for her nieces and nephews. They had grown up with little means (rice and beans were a staple), and so Ada felt obliged to share everything she had, financially and emotionally, with her siblings. When one of them struggled, whether with divorce or a bad boss, they all struggled— or at least that's what her upbringing taught her. No matter how burdened she felt by her family of origin, it never even occurred to her to let her sibs pick up their own slack. Between her job, which demanded a lot of audience engagement, and her family, Ada rarely took time out for her own well-being. She had been walking this tightrope for years, successfully—until John came along.

When I asked what she meant by "navigating this man alone," she said that in times of conflict, she could never say or do the right thing. "No matter the words I use, the active listening, the reflecting back to him what I've heard—it's chaos and turmoil. What am I doing wrong?"

The volatility between them was escalating. What she most wanted was for her pain to stop so they could return to their new couple-hood, and she could get back to business as usual. From experience, I knew that for Ada to get to the root of how she found herself in this painful relationship, we'd have to go on a fact-finding mission. We would need to uncover her unique HFC blueprint.

Your Unique HFC Blueprint

If you are familiar with my work, you have heard me refer to "blueprints" on various topics. The concept is a core part of my teaching. My first book, Boundary Boss, explored our boundary blueprints. This is the combination of influences, conscious and unconscious, that create how we relate to boundaries. Here, we will be doing the same thing, but for high-functioning codependency. In order to truly heal, we need to know how our childhood experiences are still impacting us and our relationships in adulthood, no matter how long ago they happened. Swiss psychiatrist and psychoanalyst Carl Jung asserted, "Until you make the unconscious conscious, it will direct your life and you will call it fate." What we remain unaware of can most definitely hurt us and impact the trajectory of our lives. So, let's start uncovering your blueprint.

You can think of your HFC blueprint like an architectural blueprint for a house that someone else designed long ago. It is a set of deeply ingrained beliefs, values, ideas, and behaviors that are based on your childhood experiences, culture, geography, religion, community, society, gender, race, and of course, *family*. These influences are both positive and negative. The deepest impact on how you relate to others, yourself, and the world comes from what you learned, observed, and experienced in your family of origin.

Doing a deep dive here helps you understand the factors that shape your blueprint. In unpacking the unconscious material that still exists in the "basement" or unconscious mind—and still influences your behaviors, attitudes, fears, and values—you are shining light on it, cleaning it up, and expanding your self-knowledge in the process. Bringing it up to the main part of the house (the conscious mind) gives you a chance to see it more clearly. In fact, it's your awareness that will open the door to your transformation. You can only change what you are consciously aware of.

Contemplating your experiences with the adults who raised you will provide important data points for understanding your blueprint. Like any other parental figure, yours made mistakes. They might have been straight up awful and created deep wounds that you carry to this day. Yet no matter how you fared in the parent lottery, *they* are not the point. *You* and your lived experience are.

Remember: your blueprint, your basement—at your pace.

Loving Reminder 🩶
You can unlearn dysfunctional behaviors and develop a new, more empowered skill set by understanding and changing your HFC blueprint.

BACK TO YOU
Your Unique HFC Blueprint

Examining your HFC blueprint helps you to unpack any unconscious material hiding in your "basement" that is driving your relational behaviors.

Let's reflect:

☐ Did the adults in your childhood keep commitments and act responsibly?

☐ Were either of your parents an over-giver or identified by self-sacrifice?

☐ Were either of your parents the center of the family that everyone else revolved around or tried to please?

☐ Was there honest and open communication in your family of origin?

☐ Do your relationship patterns mirror that of your parents? How?

Reflecting on these questions creates a quick snapshot of your childhood relational patterns. For the full picture, you will need to do the entire HFC blueprint exercise. When you are finished with this chapter, make time to go deeper on page 235 at the back of the book.

The Effect of Childhood Experiences on Adulthood Relationships

Many HFCs follow in their mom's self-sacrificing footsteps. If the main female caregiver in your life modeled codependent behavior, you probably thought it was normal to work overtime to take care of everyone, relegating your needs to a mere footnote that nobody ever reads. *Needs? What needs?*

Dr. Harriet Lerner, one of my heroes and the author of *The Dance of Anger: A Woman's Guide to Changing the Patterns of Intimate Relationships*, says, "Our society cultivates guilt feelings in women such that many of us still feel guilty if we are anything less than an emotional service station to others." Everyone in our life comes to us, and we fill them up with all the goodness and energy they need to keep on moving. Lather, rinse, repeat. This cycle continues—isn't that what good women do?—leaving us depleted and drained and disconnected from ourselves. That is, unless we make the radical move to break the cycle and fill our own cup. I use the word "radical" because, given that most of us were raised with such strong and predominant cultural ideals of "good" women as unfailingly kind, generous, and sometimes even compliant, it *is* radical.

When I was a teenager, I genuinely believed my single mom of four kids was perfectly happy to do all the cooking and cleaning and to wash every last dish after every meal. It wasn't until her longtime partner, Bob, pointed out our thoughtlessness one night that any of us even considered she might be more frustrated than happy with us. (We *were* teenagers, but still.) How did that situation come to be? My mother had been teaching us, via her actions, that it was appropriate for women to do all the things. Her example implicitly taught me to self-sacrifice *and* not speak up or ask for a hand when I was exhausted. It felt normal.

When we are raised with the example of putting others' needs above our own, it can create a lifetime of inherent self-abandonment and the marginalization of self. While teaching children to be kind and generous is important, a lot of us missed the addendum to that memo—*being kind and generous to others does not need to come at the exclusion of being kind and generous to* ourselves.

Beyond what we learned from our mothers and female caregivers, there are many factors, including the kind of family we grew up in, that can contribute to the development of HFC behaviors later in life.

In childhood, we watch how others behave and treat us. That modeling is how we learn to relate, and we carry it into adulthood. When Ada, my client in the volatile relationship with John, began to examine her blueprint, it became clear that what she had learned about relating from her mother was that love and pain go together. Her mother's violence often struck her and her siblings without warning. Something as minor as forgetting to close a kitchen drawer could set her mom into a tailspin of name-calling, threats, and shoving. "Nothing we ever did was good enough," she recalled with a far-off look.

Ada's role in the family was the caretaker. So, when her parents divorced, and her siblings chose to live with their father, Ada felt obligated to stay with her mother, whose abuse was escalating. Then, one day after her mother slapped her during a fight, "Something in me just broke," Ada recalled. "I thought, *no more*."

Ada packed her things, walked out the front door, and never looked back.

She was sixteen and on her own. She lived out of her car until she could figure out a plan. Eventually, she put herself through school, hustling like she'd never hustled before. Creating her own financial security acted as a cushion after so many years of not having enough and, more poignantly, feeling like *she* wasn't enough.

Yet the escalating situation with John, her new boyfriend, was clearly pointing her back in the direction of her own childhood. It was time to look back so that she could move ahead and free herself from the weight of her dysfunctional and abusive upbringing.

> **Say it with Me** 💬
> I trust myself to love, value, and choose me.

Functional vs. Dysfunctional Family Systems: Where Do You Stand?

In healthy family systems, parents foster a loving environment. There is a positive generational hierarchy in which the parents guide and create a safe container for their children to grow, explore, and develop as their own humans. Healthy families are child-focused, meaning the health, safety, and overall well-being of the kids are prioritized. There are channels for open communication; people maintain good boundaries; and adults model healthy relationships, including respecting their children's rights and preferences where appropriate.

Dysfunctional family systems, instead of being child-focused, often have a primary focus on an unhealthy dominant family member. This could be an abuser, someone with addiction issues, mental health challenges, or unhealed trauma, and can lead to children's needs not being met in healthy ways (or at all). For example, Ada's basic need for emotional safety was nonexistent due to the erratic and aggressive behavior of her mother.

In dysfunctional family systems, children are taught by example that survival and belonging mean pouring all their energy and time into others, usually their compromised caregivers, or into achieving (good grades, or excelling in sports), which can create a corrupted foundation of over-functioning later in life.

BACK TO YOU
Identifying Your Childhood Experiences

HFC behaviors can originate in families that are chaotic, abusive, or addicted, but also in families that are closed and secretive, narcissistic, enmeshed, strictly religious, perfectionistic, or authoritarian.

Below you'll find statements that describe childhood experiences that are often the foundation of codependent tendencies in adulthood. Take some time and space to go through these and mark the ones that resonate with you.

- ☐ I became a caretaker in my family of origin from a young age.

- ☐ I would do whatever I could to try to keep the peace or distract from conflict.

- ☐ In childhood I felt guilty a lot, or that things were my fault (even if they weren't).

- ☐ I had to keep secrets about my family from the rest of the world.

- ☐ I never knew what to expect in my childhood home.

- ☐ I felt like I was the only one who had a family like mine.

- ☐ I felt unworthy and inadequate.

- ☐ I always felt like I was walking on eggshells at home.

- ☐ I would often make excuses for my parents' bad behavior.

- ☐ I became my parent or caregiver's confidant. They leaned on me emotionally and told me things that were not age appropriate.

Identifying your childhood experiences is a giant first step in getting clarity on the root of your relationship patterns as an adult.

If you're ready to take a second step, choose four statements above and journal about each of them. You might do them all at once, or on consecutive days, depending on what you find.

This work can be uncomfortable and even painful. But revisiting childhood injuries helps you to honor old wounds to support your transformation. You got this, and I got you.

On the one hand, it's incredible how the little kid in you learned to adapt to your environment and any dysfunctional caregivers, molding your behavior so as not to provoke rejection, judgment, anger, or harm. If you had a parent prone to angry outbursts, you learned to adjust your language and behavior according to their mood. If you had an addicted parent, you may have learned to over-function as they under-functioned. If you had a depressed parent, you may have learned that you were responsible for lifting their mood. You may have simply been seeking the approval of a withholding parent. However you learned to please others to gain safety, love, and validation in your early life, this was your superpower for survival. What was once adaptive has become maladaptive. The little kid who needed to over-function to stay safe has become a full-fledged adult who is now unnecessarily over-functioning.

Loving Reminder 🩶
We can't possibly be expected to know what no one taught us, and the good news is, it's never too late to learn.

Understanding Trauma

Childhood trauma comes in many forms: physical, psychological, sexual, and verbal abuse along with witnessing violence and being emotionally neglected. Untreated trauma has a lasting impact on our ability to function optimally in life. Understanding how past trauma may be affecting us physically, emotionally, and mentally is integral for healing in the here and now.

In the past, we associated trauma with a major, life-threatening event. Those who were "allowed" to claim trauma were military veterans and ER docs, survivors of fires and other natural disasters, car crashes, and violent crimes. Nowadays, we think about trauma more expansively—and that's a good thing for our individual and collective well-being.

In his book *The Myth of Normal: Trauma, Illness, and Healing in a Toxic Culture*, physician and addiction expert Dr. Gabor Maté offers an illuminating definition of trauma: "Trauma is not what happens to you but what happens inside you." Trauma is the way in which we carry events and experiences, and how these events and experiences live on inside of us, sometimes for decades.

Maté believes that those who have not experienced trauma are exceptions to the rule in our society. Most of us have some kind of "little-t trauma" in our backgrounds, meaning we've sustained enduring scars from so-called casual happenings, such as being bullied by peers or ridiculed by an otherwise well-intentioned parent. His message is that if something seemingly small has left a mark on your psyche, it's impact may not be small. Little-t trauma might also stem from a parent who doesn't outright abuse or neglect you but still fails to give you the kind of encouragement, validation, and love that you needed to feel safe and secure. Being emotionally neglected, too—not seen and loved for who we are, not having our emotions validated and supported—is also its own form of trauma.

Understanding the impact of your own past trauma is the path to healing it.

There are three main trauma responses—fight, flight, freeze. These are the body's physiological defenses to perceived threats. How we react or respond to feeling threatened now is informed by our past experiences. We prepare to fight, we run away, or we play dead. More recently, therapist Pete Walker, also introduced *fawning*, which we can think of as extreme placating or appeasing. He says, "Fawn types seek safety by merging with the wishes, needs, and demands of others. They act as if they believe that the price of admission to any relationship is the forfeiture of all their needs, rights, preferences, and boundaries."

As with the other trauma responses, we can default to fawning when we feel afraid for our emotional and physical safety and well-being, sending our nervous system into dysregulated free fall and prompting a cascade of high adrenaline and other stress hormones to surge throughout our bodies.

The important thing to understand is that our trauma responses can be triggered unconsciously and in response to situations that are not actually life-threatening. Our bodies are just trying to keep ourselves safe based on what we've experienced in the past. To change these automatic responses, we have to process the past trauma (I recommend seeking the support of a trauma specialist to address untreated trauma when possible) and calm our nervous systems. Breathwork, meditation, and yoga can be excellent ways to get back into our bodies, one slow exhale at a time. (In part 2 we'll cover strategies and tips for nervous system regulation.)

In my clinical experience, many HFCs who endured childhood trauma or neglect tend to minimize its impact. Often, this is because they are very capable and high functioning, handling a high-power job or a demanding family or social life. They say, "I'm fine. I've made a good life. How bad could it have been?"

A clue that all is not well comes when I ask them how they *feel* and they honestly don't know. In contrast, they almost never have a problem telling me what they *think* about things. Not knowing how or what we *feel* can be a sign of disassociation from our body and lived experiences and can be a sign of trauma. By staying in this pattern, we are unconsciously denying ourselves the full spectrum of our experiences and emotions by suppressing parts of ourselves that need our attention. Then, the pattern of tolerating mistreatment can get repeated in our careers, relationships, and friendships—and we have no idea why this trouble keeps following us around.

Repeating Relationship Realities

In Ada's case, when John showed up with a volatility eerily similar to her mother's, it potentially indicated that something from her past was being played out in the present. John's hypercritical, nothing-you-do-is-good-enough attitude was unconsciously familiar to her. I call it a Repeating Relationship Reality because it mirrored her early experiences that she'd worked so hard to leave behind.

It can be confounding and more than a little depressing to find yourself replaying the same unsatisfying interactions, leading to the same undesirable outcomes. And it is the way we are wired. Humans seek comfort in the familiar. They can even feel compelled to repeat dramatic or—according to Freud—traumatic experiences. Freud referred to the latter phenomenon as "repetition compulsion." As a therapist, I see both positive and negative childhood experiences being unconsciously repeated in adult relationships. When we repeat the negative experiences, it's as if the child in us is seeking a do-over by getting into a relationship with a partner who has some similar traits to a difficult parent. Unconsciously, Ada may have been seeking the happy ending with John that she never got to experience with her mother. The kid thinks, *This time it will be different. I will be good/smart/pretty/interesting enough to gain and keep their love, affection, and attention.* Sadly, much of the time, this effort is doomed to fail because, as part of the repetition compulsion, we are specifically choosing and attracting individuals with deep limitations and problems as was the case with our original relationships. To create a better outcome, we need to understand and honor our childhood experiences and the unconscious material in the basement of our minds.

The Shame Game

Childhood traumas, big and small, can create shame. As far as emotions go, shame is the heaviest and can be the most devastating. Whatever the source, shame causes us to hold ourselves in low regard for being somehow different. The effects can be far-reaching, corrosive, and devastating. Shame has a much more toxic effect on our life when we don't even realize that we're carrying it.

Many HFCs tend to have a convincing "game face"—*nothing to see here*—so naturally shame stays hidden, often from themselves (mine sure did). When you're a highly capable person, the last thing you want to admit is feeling like you are defective at the most basic level of your being. Yet it's critical to bring hidden shame to light because it can negatively affect our decision-making, as well as how we relate and behave in our lives.

Brené Brown's definition of shame captures this damage to the self. She says, "The intensely painful feeling or experience of believing that we are flawed and therefore unworthy of love and belonging—something we've experienced, done, or failed to do— makes us unworthy of connection." This feeling of unworthiness naturally feeds straight into HFC behaviors in adulthood.

Shame is sometimes confused with guilt, but they are not the same. The easiest distinction is this: healthy guilt is an experience

(*I did something wrong*), while shame is an identity (*I am wrong*). When awash in shame, we might feel inherently flawed and irrevocably broken.

With guilt, the focus is on a behavior we may feel remorseful about. For example, you broke your friend's confidence or snapped at someone. As human beings, we all make choices outside of our integrity sometimes. No matter how long it takes to process healthy guilt, we can apologize, and ultimately, our self-esteem remains intact. In contrast, shame cuts straight to the core of our self-esteem. *Something is wrong with me.* We feel we have to hide who we are at the most fundamental level.

> ### Loving Reminder 🖤
> My past mistakes do not determine my future. I do.

Unhealed Shame

Unhealed shame can show up in our lives as perfectionism, workaholism, and over-achieving. The constant bid for external validation can be an attempt to avoid deep feelings of inherent unworthiness that we may be carrying around within us. Unhealed shame can also show up in our finances, like it did for Ada, whose feelings of unworthiness drove her to over-give financially to her loved ones. Unhealed shame can flare in the tendency to downplay our achievements and blessings, out of fear of overshadowing others. A person with a healthy self-regard can share good news openly and freely, while someone who is burdened by shame plays small, not wanting to become a target of someone else's jealousy. That way, they stay safe, but also stuck.

Perfectionism. Perfectionism often comes with unrealistic and unrelenting high standards, for ourselves and everyone else but there is more to it. At its core, it is a way to avoid the thing that many HFCs fear the most: failure. When perfectionism is our driving MO, we're always going the extra mile to be thoughtful. We pull off remarkable feats, like organizing the best dinner parties, sparing no detail. Perfectionism can also inspire rumination, repetitive thinking, or dwelling on negative aspects of an experience. We cannot bear it when life does not go as we planned (in other words, we are not good at *rolling with the punches*) and so we focus our mental energy, not on the big picture, or the many things that went amazingly well, but that lone, off-script detail we couldn't control. This is a recipe for unhappiness, both within ourselves (because we're low-key telling ourselves we're not good enough as we are) and within our relationships (because no one likes to be criticized or feel like they're not meeting our over-the-top standards).

HFCs who exhibit perfectionism are committed to "the right way" to do life—a mindset that creates rigidity in thinking and leaves little room for spontaneity, creativity, or genuine presence.

BACK TO YOU
Three Steps to Ease Shame

Shame thrives in silence and judgment. The antidote is self-compassion, self-empathy, and selective transparency (selecting when, and with whom, you share vulnerable details).

Below are three actions you can take to start freeing yourself from shame:

1. If you experience an upswelling of shame, take as many breaths as you need to calm your mind and body. This will help you to be able to respond from your current situation (how things are today), not from the pain of an unresolved injury in the past.

2. Monitor your thoughts for any self-shaming language you may have internalized from parents or caregivers. Can you distinguish between your own self-talk and thoughts that were planted by someone else? This knowledge will help you stop the self-shaming cycle.

3. If you make a mistake, use compassionate (instead of shaming) language to soothe yourself. Reassure yourself that it's okay to be human.

Revealing these parts of yourself honestly is imperative for your healing—and for developing genuine self-confidence. Anything you cannot tolerate looking at can powerfully direct your behavior. While your unconscious mind may be protecting you from vulnerability, this act of hiding also drains you of precious energy and diminishes your ability to show up with a clear and coherent sense of who you are. (You're amazing, btw.)

Tapping into her courage, Ada uncovered her blueprint. She realized that she was harboring deep shame. That shame (plus a whole lot of guilt) prompted her to feel eternally indebted to everyone around her—even though *she* was the one giving the financial and emotional support. Her mother's abuse had left its mark. Her underlying belief was that she was unworthy; she was compelled to try to compensate by over-giving. From unpacking her blueprint, she also realized this feeling of unworthiness stemmed not only from her mother's psychological and physical abuse, but also from her father's absence of protection. Where once she had idealized her father, now she saw things differently. This new awareness brought up a lot of intense feelings.

Deep down, the part of her that felt deserving of her boyfriend, John's, rotten treatment was changing. While she didn't end the relationship immediately, she couldn't unknow what she had discovered about him and their connection, and was biding her time until she could make a plan to get out safely. In the interim, she chose to redirect much of her energy away from John and toward healing.

"That's what I want," Ada said, "to choose healing. So now what do I do?"

Ada *had* been doing her best to survive and do right by others—and now she was committed to do right by herself, too. This meant constructing a new relational blueprint that considered her preferences and needs first, no matter who she was relating to.

Integrating the Past

Regardless of what your blueprint revealed about your childhood experiences, the foundation of your healing is in *integrating* what happened. You need to honor these experiences, memories, and feelings with generous doses of self-acceptance and self-kindness.

You deserve to be loved and cherished for who you are. That's as true now as it was when you were a child. Connecting with old emotions of isolation, fear, shame, and grief may feel daunting at first. But the reality is, once you can invite these feelings into conscious awareness with great compassion for the kid in you who may have gone through some seriously hard stuff, you can begin to re-parent yourself, showing yourself the love, care, and respect that you are worthy of.

In part 2 of this book, we'll dive more deeply into specific self-care and self-love tips, but for now, start by being as kind to yourself as you are to others. When it comes to our own rules of engagement, the standards HFCs set for ourselves are rough. We don't naturally have a lot of compassion for ourselves, and this can seriously curtail the quality of our lives. It's much easier to embrace change, take risks, and grow when we're not being our own worst critic. When you catch yourself being self-critical, stop, notice, take a breath, and redirect yourself to a different thought. For now, that's enough.

> ### Loving Reminder
> Every experience—from your injuries to your awakenings—is a
> golden thread in the tapestry of your unique and beautiful life.

Ada created her freedom by making healing her number one priority. Once she acknowledged and honored her childhood wounds through the blueprint process, she was ready to make some bold moves. She lovingly let her family know that her financial support could not continue as it had. Where she had standing agreements (like helping her sister with a monthly car payment), she created a wind-down plan, so her sister had notice that she would take over the payments and Ada had peace of mind. It was a huge deal for Ada to stop being over-responsible for others and focus on herself. Her sister gracefully accepted these terms, thanked her for her help all these years, and then proceeded to step up to the plate and is now self-sufficient and thriving. Once she made this decision, Ada was surprised to see that in all her over-functioning and über-resilience, she had been hoping that someone would come along and save her from the pain of her childhood. At first, this was hard for Ada to digest, but in time, she began to gather up and build her inner resources, so that she could confidently, joyfully, and eagerly save herself. Things started to transform the moment she turned her attention away from her chaotic relationship and began pouring her energy and attention into herself.

Ada dove deep into looking at her relationships with fresh eyes and concluded that any relationship not built on principles of healthy respect and mutuality was not for her. This led her to safely, strategically, and permanently end her relationship with John. Marking her newfound freedom, Ada took a long road trip, just her and her dogs.

> ### *Loving Reminder* 🖤
> No matter what your HFC blueprint reveals, you can
> learn to re-parent yourself, heal your childhood injuries,
> and create healthy relationships in adulthood.

A year later, she found a group of folks she could be genuinely vulnerable with, and today she is no longer driven by hidden shame and unhealed childhood scars. She's honest with her online audience about what she experiences and has created an emotionally supportive community. The energy she's regained by not being overly focused on taking care of her family, and not acting from unacknowledged guilt or shame, has resulted in new creative projects and ideas. Along the way, she's been devoted to her healing work, seeking out modalities that really lift her up and out of the lower vibrations from where she came. Recently, I asked Ada how she was doing and she simply said, "I'm in love—with life."

► TAKE ACTION ◄

- **Top of Mind.** Throughout the day, pay attention to the cues from your body. Ask yourself, "What do I need right now? Do I need to stretch, breathe deeply, or move? Am I hungry, thirsty, tired?" Then, take the time to give yourself what you need.

- **Take Care.** Spend a few moments every day repeating the following affirmation to yourself: *My past experiences do not define me. I release shame and joyfully embrace and accept all of me.*

- **Go Deeper: HFC Blueprint.** This exercise will help you connect the dots of how your past experiences influence your present-day relational behaviors. Go to page 235 in the "Go Deeper" section of the book to do the complete HFC blueprint exercise.

CHAPTER 4

HFC Relationships

How You Relate to Others

OFTEN, THE WAKE-UP call to our HFC tendencies comes when one of our relationships goes through a challenge or even a breakdown. For Dina, a sixty-two-year-old client who came to me because she couldn't get out of a funk, that moment seemed to arrive out of the blue.

A full-time pediatric nurse, Dina was used to taking care of everyone and everything. In addition to caring for her patients at crucial moments in their lives, Dina's daughter had come to live with Dina and her husband, often leaving her two small children in Dina's care while she went to work. In her twenty-nine-year marriage, the division of labor had not been equal, with Dina spearheading the grocery shopping, cleaning, and cooking, while Ed, her unemployed husband, sat comfortably in his recliner, catching up on news and sports with a few beers every night. Ed's long-term hypertension and respiratory disease gave him a hall pass when it came to helping out. As Dina rushed around her house, she'd occasionally look at him and think, *must be nice.* But for the most part, she accepted this dynamic, partly because this was just what women in her generation were raised to expect— doing too much for others and not getting much help in return. While Dina and her friends would sometimes complain about the futility of trying to get their spouses to pitch in more, no one imagined that their relationships could look otherwise. In fact, a lot of times after hanging out with her friends, Dina would listen to other stories and think, *Thank God Ed's not like that!*

In therapy, when I asked Dina what she was hoping for, she replied, "Honestly? Not to be exhausted every second of my life." Talking about her situation brought her new insights and relief, and soon, she felt a growing intolerance of the status quo. After getting off long night shifts, seeing her husband's half-empty cereal bowl in the sink started to grate. Now, entering the bathroom to find an empty toilet paper roll really made her mad.

One night, as she was on her way out for her night shift, Ed said, "Hey, babe, can you make me scrambled eggs before you go?"

She sighed. "Actually, I'm tired and looking at a long night," she said. "Can you make the eggs?"

She didn't plan to say this, but the words materialized as if by magic.

Ed, however, did not find Dina's request magical. "Oh, sure. I'll make it myself," he said, clearly irritated.

If Dina wasn't so annoyed, she might have laughed at what happened next. Ed, who had lived in this house the exact same number of years as Dina, started opening and shutting cabinets, looking for a pan. *How does he not know where the pans are?* she thought. While Dina watched, he opened the refrigerator door, scanning the shelves. "Do you use butter?" he asked. "Would you also use oil?"

The door was open so long it started beeping.

"What's that?" he said, looking alarmed. "What kind of cheese would you put in eggs—cheddar?"

Good lord. Looking at Ed feign such helplessness in his own kitchen, Dina walked over, grabbed the butter from his hands, and said, "Never mind. I'll do it."

There's got to be a better way, she thought.

When we finally take a long look at our patterns in relationships, we start to see how it's never just that one pan of scrambled eggs, that one time we inconvenienced ourselves, that one relationship. This long-overdue interpersonal revision will affect every aspect of how you relate to others—including how you set boundaries, the balance of giving and taking, and where you're unconsciously driven by a need to manage those around you.

When you're an HFC, you are *all about* the relationships in your life. Healthy relationships are built on *mutuality*—relatively equal effort in giving and taking. But if you're an HFC, you are likely giving more than you are taking.

The first step in changing deeply entrenched relationship dynamics is seeing the dynamic clearly. Become aware of it without beating yourself up. Witness with neutrality, non-judgment, and self-compassion. Be an observer, not a drill sergeant. Patience helps a lot. My hope is that, by educating yourself on these relational dynamics, you, too, will recognize, *there really is a better way.*

BACK TO YOU
Take a Relationship Inventory

Taking a relationship inventory will provide a precise snapshot of your current relationship patterns. Set aside a little time to gather information and honestly assess your important relationships, one at a time.

Consider the following three areas and make a list, following the example below. Then, fill in your answers. Aim to list at least five close relationships. If you have time, list up to ten.

- **The WHO:** Can include family, friends, frenemies, romantic partners, siblings, boss, coworkers, etc.

□ **The BEHAVIOR:** Can include behaviors that cause imbalance and unwanted feelings, including over-giving, rejecting help, passive-aggressive communication, covert or overt control, etc.

□ **The FEELINGS:** Can include resentment, obligation, guilt, anger, feeling underappreciated or unimportant, etc.

1. Who_____

2. Behavior _____

3. Feeling _____

This assessment will act as a guide to which relationships in your life need the most attention.

HFC Relationship Issues

When you start to examine your relationships, you may see that many of them have things in common. You might feel overly responsible for keeping the relationships going or repeatedly attract emotionally unavailable partners. The problems may express differently in each unique situation, but there will most likely be similarities, including disordered boundaries (which we will cover in chapter 8), hyper-independence, difficulty expressing or allowing for vulnerability, and unsatisfying sexual intimacy. Everything is worth looking at.

Hyper-independence. Many HFCs default to hyper-independence, relying primarily on themselves. This is especially true of those who experienced abuse or neglect as a child. Hyper-independence may seem admirable to observers—*wow, she doesn't need anyone!* But it's actually more like, *wow, she doesn't trust anyone.*

Healthy independence says, "I got this, and I will ask for and accept help when I need it." Hyper-independence says, "I got this, and it's easier for me to have my own back. That way I can avoid being a burden to or being disappointed by others." Hyper-independence can be an extreme and sometimes damaging form of self-reliance that can result in isolation, unfulfilling relationships, and doing way too much for other people, while never expecting reciprocity. Hyper-independence can also be an attempt at self-protection.

If we look back at our original blueprints, we may find that having needs was a scary prospect. Maybe we didn't have adults who were equipped to help us. Or perhaps asking and receiving help created unsafe conditions. In adulthood, that could translate to, "I'd rather do it myself." As a result of hyper-independence, we often feel alone, even in our closest relationships. We have unwittingly placed ourselves in the position of always doing for others and often expecting little in return or outright rejecting offers of help. Inevitably, the folks in our lives will stop offering. When this happens, we may feel unimportant, or taken advantage of. We might think that the other people are acting entitled, forgetting that, in essence, we trained them to believe that we don't want or need their help or consideration.

My own hyper-independence came into full view when I first started dating my husband, Vic. I'd known him for a long time as a friend before we fell in love, and every step of the way, his behavior matched his words. When I told Bev that I was freaked out because Vic offered to do so much for me, she asked, "Why is that?"

When I explained that I didn't want to be that vulnerable, she made me dig deeper—"and why is that?"

"Well, I'm already in love with him," I explained, "so he now has the power to annihilate me." Sounds dramatic, yet those were the exact words I used. I had spent so many years in my hyper-independent groove that surrendering to what was organically unfolding between us felt life-threatening. I literally thought, *If this guy betrays me, I might just die.* Over time, as Vic consistently showed up in loving and reliable ways, I stopped waiting for the other shoe to drop.

Difficulty Being Vulnerable. Telling the truth of our most tender emotions can be very hard for those of us who are HFCs. Since messy emotions don't fit with our "together" self-image, we may ignore or bypass how we genuinely feel.

We may find it easier to resort to anger when our feelings get hurt. We want to be strong, not seen as "weak." As a result, we may deny or repress our hurt feelings because that makes us vulnerable to another person. For so many of us, being vulnerable in our early life didn't work out well—it led to being punished, ridiculed, or shamed.

In the beginning, when you start honoring deeper (and perhaps gnarlier) feelings, you may get a flood of emotions and responses, such as spontaneous tears. This can be jarring when you are used to being in full control of yourself. Yet getting in touch with your true feelings and risking vulnerability is key to creating genuine, rewarding relationships.

> ### Say It with Me 💬
> I deserve love, care, and consideration and choose
> to engage in relationships that reflect my worth.

Limited or Unsatisfying Intimacy. As HFCs, we tend to be averse to emotional vulnerability and surrender, and our intimate lives can suffer as a result. We don't want to lose control, and that inhibits our ability to be fully present. Raw, unscripted intimacy cannot happen when we have a driving need to be (and stay) in charge.

This keeps us comfortable—and disconnected from our own needs and desires.

HFCs are skilled at checking off the boxes, and for many, sex is a box. *Did we do it once this week? Yes, great. Everybody satisfied? Excellent. We're good.* Societally, it's been so deeply ingrained that men need sex that we may go above and beyond to make sure that happens. *As long as they're happy, I'm happy.* But we lose out when we approach sexual encounters in such a rigid way. We miss out on the good stuff, especially genuine sexual connection and satisfaction.

I had a client who lied about having orgasms with her husband for fifteen years. Why? Because she wanted him to feel good, and she recognized that an important part of his good experience was knowing that she had a good experience. Of course, from the outside looking in, the logic breaks down. If you both like knowing the other person enjoys your shared sex life, then wouldn't you work as a team to meet that goal?

My client viewed sex with her husband as a job to manage so there was no room to be a teammate. Her decision to lie took away his right to know what was actually happening for her. You can't have a genuine connection with someone and be managing them simultaneously. Eventually, my client told her partner the truth and he felt hurt, angry, and betrayed. They got into couples therapy together, but it took years to rebuild the trust that was broken.

In the bedroom and beyond, many HFCs will "take one for the team." In reality, no one asked for that. What may seem to an HFC like self-sacrificing behavior that benefits all, can, in fact, hurt people—including themselves.

As you can see, unchecked HFC tendencies in relationships keep us siloed away from the people we care about. They block us from experiencing the richness and rewards of genuine connection. It's like we build ourselves a tower and lock ourselves in it.

BACK TO YOU
Practicing Authentic Communication

☐ Make a list of things that bother you that you haven't shared with your partner. They can be big or small, but they should be things you've never told them. Where have you not been completely open about what you really want, think, or feel?

☐ Set aside some time with your partner to have a conversation. Pick one issue to share. It's okay—and honestly, so much more effective—to go slowly, one thing at a time. You don't have to get through your entire list in one sitting. You can say, "I want to do something different," or "I want to break out of X, Y, Z." Just gently and lovingly assert yourself, without blame or shame.

Once you begin to see a positive change, your confidence and courage will continue to build, and you can move into another area on your list. This exercise can be useful in any relationship with two willing participants.

What's Behind the Need to Control

As we've established, HFCs are compelled to control others, not out of malice but in an attempt to avoid conflict and keep the peace. This control can manifest as overprotectiveness to shield others from harm or failure, often justifying their controlling behavior as being in the other person's best interest. It can also appear as micromanaging, where they obsess over details, or manipulation, where they subtly coerce others into following their plans. The bid for control may be obvious (*I'm going to call up my sister and give her a script so she can tell off her toxic boss*), or it might be subtle (*I'm going to replace all the pasta with quinoa for "health reasons"*). Either way, trying to exert control means we're leaving our side of the street behind and crossing into the no-fly zone of other people's business.

No matter how well-intentioned, controlling behavior is usually fear-based. With my sister, Jenna, whose story I shared in chapter 2, my fear propelled me to controlling behaviors that looked like spending hours on the phone with her when I had a demanding full-time job and three stepkids who needed the best of me. Though I didn't realize that what I was doing was controlling, I would inevitably become frustrated when another week passed without Jenna taking my advice. (Consistent frustration with another person's choices can be a telltale sign that a desire to control is present.)

The goal is to move away from the management of others and toward interdependence. That is where each person has the right to and feels free to negotiate for their own needs, desires, wants, and preferences. There is a mutuality of trust and respect. Interdependency in practice is a healthy form of dependency that strengthens relationships. What's required to change is a willingness to look at yourself and your own behavior. Look with radical curiosity instead of judgment. This includes self-judgment of how you are functioning as well as judging others.

Before I was in recovery for HFC, I would often:

- Blame the other person for taking advantage of me, rather than understanding my own role in putting myself in that position.

- Refuse to accept help from others, but rush to fix everything for everyone else.

- Turn someone perfectly capable and competent into an under-functioner. Then, because they got conditioned by my over-functioning behavior, they'd step back and let me do all the things and I'd become resentful.

- End up feeling angry, unknown, used, and sometimes kicked to the curb.

While it's largely an unconscious drive, the need to control negatively affects our relationships. And try as we might, we cannot effectively protect, direct, or control anyone else. On top of that, our efforts will not bring us the calm, peace, or connection we're looking for.

So why do we try to control people? It boils down to our inability to tolerate our own discomfort about the other person's discomfort. We shut it down by taking action/diverting/fixing/consoling, etc.—whatever it takes to avoid having someone else be angry, unhappy, hurt, or upset.

You might be thinking, *Okay, so all I have to do is learn to tolerate others' discomfort?* Yes, *and* a worthier mission is to learn to tolerate *your own*.

Loving Reminder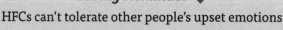
HFCs can't tolerate other people's upset emotions
which compels us to attempt to *fix* them.

When we're in control mode, we can also inadvertently depersonalize the situation (and the other person), which is the opposite of what we say we want. Said another way, we can become so focused on achieving *our* desired outcomes for *them* that we lose sight of the other person altogether.

If you're *that* friend who knows *exactly* what other people *should* be doing, it's possible your friends and loved ones actually fear your interference or disapproval. People around you may be walking on eggshells, worrying about your involvement, judgments, or even wrath. We don't want our friends and family to be scared of our judgments or criticism. We want them to know that we love, care, and support them. And we want to be loved, cared for and supported in return. This requires trust—trusting ourselves, and trusting them.

Enabling and Under-Functioning

The HFC need to control and over-function can enable and inspire chronic under-functioning in others. We teach others that we will manage their stuff so they don't have to. This is a form of enabling.

We commonly think of the term "enabler" in the context of addicted relationships—for example, a mother giving her drug-addicted son money, essentially closing her eyes to his serious problem. He doesn't have to feel the pain of his own actions, and his mother can stay in her bubble of denial.

When over-functioning outside the context of addiction, many HFCs do not recognize themselves as enablers. And yet they are.

Codependency and the enabling behaviors that go with it inadvertently prolong undesirable situations, thanks to a driving need to make sure that nothing bad happens. As we've illustrated, this is faulty reasoning because controlling others in the external world will not calm the storm within—it's your job to create and hold onto your inner peace. If you continue to clean up the fallout from a loved one's bad choices, they may never hit their bottom and find the inner grit they need to make serious changes in their lives. Preventing others from facing the real consequences of their problematic behavior creates long-term issues. There's no impetus to change. In working with couples in my therapy practice, I have also seen a perfectly capable person *turned into* an under-functioner because their partner continued to insist that they "had things covered" which ultimately created resentment for both parties.

Emotional Labor

The tendency to over-function can result in defaulting to doing way more emotional labor than others in their lives. *Emotional labor* refers to the invisible, unpaid work that so many women do in order to keep everything afloat—at home, work, and in life in general—everything from writing thank you notes to weekly calls with their mother-in-law because their partner doesn't have the time (or desire). This form of invisible work can be taken to the extreme, especially when we're telling ourselves that it's just easier if we handle whatever it is that needs to be handled. Many of us have simply become accustomed to shouldering more than our fair share. When we begin to see the pattern, it can make us very mad, or very sad, or both.

BACK TO YOU
How Much Emotional Labor Are You Doing?

If you feel like there's an unequal balance of emotional labor in any aspect of your life, ask yourself these questions:

- ☐ In what relationships are you doing more emotional labor than you need to?

- ☐ Where are you the point person for all the emotional caretaking? Make a list.

- ☐ In what relationships are you over-functioning? Who might be under-functioning as a result?

If emotional and other responsibilities are evenly distributed in your relationships, great! If not, it's time to reassess and have some conversations to reset and rebalance.

When Dina, my client married to the reluctant egg chef, began to take stock of the underlying relational dynamics, it became clear to her that she was an over-functioner and Ed, her husband, was an under-functioner. Her focus in recent years had been on her own finite energy levels. As she aged, she did not have the limitless bandwidth she once had.

"When we got married," she said, "it felt like it was us against the world. Ed was not always this apathetic. He used to bound downstairs in the morning, make me my coffee, and bring it to me in bed. He hasn't done that in . . . I don't know . . . at least a couple decades?"

When I asked her if she could pinpoint a shift, she said, "Hmmm . . . well, I guess it happened around the time we had our oldest child. For financial reasons, I had to pick up more shifts starting when the baby was six months old. It's all a blur, really, but I was working on some kind of autopilot because it was just easier for me to handle everything."

"If you could guess, what do you think changed for Ed?"

Dina thought for a moment. "You know, I remember him becoming needier around that time. As I was doing it all, I'd not only left myself out of the equation, but him, too."

When Dina rejected Ed's attempts to help and connect, he eventually gave up. In our next session, Dina shared that she talked to Ed about this time. He said, "We went from being a dynamic duo to you being a one-woman show."

Eventually, Ed even admitted that initially, part of his reluctance to pitch in was not wanting to be criticized because Dina always had a better or more efficient way to get something done, but he also hoped his inaction would get her attention. And as his health challenges worsened so did his effort. Then somewhere along the way, this became their new norm.

> *Loving Reminder* 🖤
> Mutuality and interdependence are the
> foundations for healthy relationships.

Summoning her courage, Dina eventually told Ed, "I can't do this anymore. I'm tired. We have to find a better way."

Ed agreed with Dina. The more Ed and Dina were honest with each other, the more they each came to appreciate what the experience had been like for the other. Ed felt emasculated because Dina was so efficient and earning the lion's share of income. He'd become down and depressed before he got sick, and then his illness created an excuse to under-function. None of it made him feel particularly great about himself—or life.

Slowly and surely, they figured out concrete ways to balance the scales. Ed offered to manage the grocery list and do the shopping. If Dina was in a tough work stretch, the responsibility for taking their grandkids to school or doctor's appointments fell to Ed. Day by day, they felt more like the dynamic duo they once were.

The Cost of Our HFC on Other People

Now it's time to look at how our high-functioning codependency affects the other party—not what we *think* we are doing for them, but how they may be experiencing our words and actions. The cost of our HFC-ness on others involves some degree of denying them their autonomy—the right to have feelings, the right to struggle, the right to wade in uncertain waters and find their way, the right to show up for others as they wish, and the right to make their own mistakes. Without intending to, we may be violating others' boundaries, a feature that is present in each of the costs we're exploring: emotional invalidation, hyper-positivity, auto-advice giving, and managing others' behavior.

Emotional Invalidation. Emotional invalidation might look like dismissing someone's valid expression or point of view because it's hard to tolerate. For example, you jump in to fix a friend's problems instead of witnessing her in her pain. Or maybe your mother expresses disappointment because you couldn't make it home for the holidays, and you cut her off by saying, "Think about what we're going to cook together next year, Mom!"—a response that steamrolls over her valid feelings about what is happening for her right now.

While unintentional, emotional invalidation can have some painful consequences. It can make our loved ones feel ashamed for their human emotions and also block us from truly connecting with them.

Consider times when you, too, have been on the receiving end of emotional invalidation. You call up a pal needing to vent, and she comes back at you with, "Your anger isn't helping. You should focus on X, Y, Z." Does this response make you feel seen or understood in your time of need? It does not.

To nurture and create strong, healthy relationships, emotional validation that flows both ways must be present. Learning to validate others' emotional realities means accepting that they're in whatever kind of moment they're in. There's no need to put a shiny bow on it or try to covertly manipulate or manage the situation so we feel better.

When we start to be more attuned to our need to avoid discomfort and see how it can result in unintentional emotional invalidation of others we truly care about, we have the awareness we need to make different choices.

Hyper-positivity. Looking on the bright side of life is admirable when it's genuine. But hyper-positivity is not completely sincere—it happens when we refuse to sit with another person's frustration or pain and instead shine a light on "the bright side." We might even become what I call silver-lining detectives, clinging to the most optimistic of perspectives, even when it's inappropriate and unhelpful. (*God never gives you more than you can handle. Everything happens for a reason.*)

Hyper-positivity is a form of emotional invalidation. If you are prone to sprinkling rainbows over someone else's fears, worries, or sadness, what you're really doing is trying to make your discomfort about their reality go away.

The end result of hyper-positivity is that the other person feels less like a pal and more like a problem you just "solved." What's lost for both of you is a chance to truthfully connect around real-life feelings and situations.

Auto-advice Giving. We covered auto-advice giving in chapter 2. Now let's look at it from the POV of someone on the receiving end.

Your immediate impulse to offer guidance will elicit a whole spectrum of reactions. Some folks will tolerate your fix-it ways, accepting that this is part of how you show your love and care. Others will let your unsolicited "how-to" strategies roll right off their back. If they, too, are HFCs, your auto-advice may annoy them, but it will not surprise them because it goes both ways. They are just as likely to immediately give you *their* two cents on what you should do in all situations, as you are. Others will be grateful for you listing a five-point plan to help them clean up a mess.

In the worst-case scenario (which is more common than you might think), some folks will be downright offended by your auto-advice because it's a clear bypass of their own lived experience and inner wisdom.

When we're in pain, all we want is to know that someone cares, and that we're not alone in our foxhole. We do not need a definitive answer to our problem, especially because no one else can possibly know it. When someone veers into auto-advice giving, both parties can wind up feeling alone and alienated, with neither person feeling heard nor seen.

Managing Other People's Behavior. As HFCs, we often find ourselves trying to manage others' behavior—a form of meddling. But no one likes to be managed. People want to be trusted and respected, not directed.

Let's say you have a friend who seems kind of down in the dumps. You call a mutual friend to give them the heads up. "Betty's not doing okay, and I thought you might want to know." Nothing wrong with that, right? Depending on the relationship, no, but only if it stops there. Often, HFCs will call the friend, give them the heads up, and then not be able to resist following up to ensure execution, such as, "Did you reach out? How did she sound? Is she okay?" Being on the receiving end of this kind of controlling behavior can be off-putting.

Healthy vs. Unhealthy Relationships

There's a cracked pot for every cracked lid—and that can be good for our healing.

As an HFC, your partner's cracks (their particular faults, weaknesses, or issues) may be irresistible to you. You can't help but want to dig in, fix, and help heal. If you've come up with a whole dissertation on their mommy issues, you may be thinking, *They just have to heal that and we'll be fine.* Your assessment of their stuff isn't necessarily wrong; rather, the wrongness lies in believing this is your job. If you try to present your unsolicited case study of their life, well, expect that to be met with resistance, resentment, or both.

A healthier line of thinking is, *What are my issues that fit so perfectly with their set of issues?*

This is important. When we are preoccupied with the other person, we are ignoring ourselves. Anytime you find yourself thinking,

I don't want them to think X, or *I don't want them to feel Y,* that's your cue to get back on your own side of the street. So what if they think or feel whatever they do? They're entitled to their experience, and more importantly, how they might respond can give you vital information about them.

> ### Loving Reminder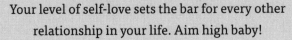
> Your level of self-love sets the bar for every other
> relationship in your life. Aim high baby!

For many HFCs, healthy dependence—where both people give and receive encouragement, support, and practical help—can be challenging, like it was for me with Vic. It can stir up an overwhelming fear of losing control. Yet when we stay in our control-driven behavioral patterns, we deny ourselves and our people a closer connection. Even if changing this dynamic seems daunting, it is completely possible, one next right action at a time.

New Beginnings

The more Dina and Ed started to relate to one another again as true partners, the more they began to talk about their long-term goals. Yes, there was a better balance in the division of labor in her marriage, yet Dina was still bone-tired. Having her daughter and their grandchildren living with them had become stressful and was starting to feel unsustainable. "This isn't how we imagined our golden years," Dina explained.

After taking care of others for years, she deserved a break. Both Dina and Ed were also aware of their dwindling time on the planet, especially with Ed's medical condition. How could they find more enjoyment in each other and life? Stepping out of autopilot had enabled them to think more about long-term plans. Ed brought up their dream of moving somewhere warm, so that the winter months were more enjoyable. Dina was intrigued by this idea, but still felt the burden of responsibility for her adult daughter and grandchildren.

It took some time for her to accept that she had every right to end the grind and create plans with Ed to savor the last act of their lives. After working so hard for so many years, it wasn't selfish of her to want to have time with her husband instead of caregiving for her adult daughter and grandkids. As much as she loved her family, the over-functioning had dampened the experience of being a grand-mother because she was so tired all the time and bogged down by the obligations of the situation.

Eventually, Dina and Ed called a family meeting and told their daughter that they were planning on retiring to North Carolina, where they had plenty of friends. They made it clear that they'd plan visits and could take the kids for school and summer vaca-tions here and there. Their daughter was supportive of this new vision of their lives and grateful for all they'd already done for her and her family.

Dina's story illustrates how our breakdown moments can be breakthroughs, leading to healthy changes in all our relationships. You, too, can back off the inadvertent controlling, enabling, and managing of others and begin to foster more mutuality and healthy dependence in your relationships. When we practice staying in our own lane, it is amazing how much of ourselves—our true selves—we are able to connect with and recapture. And that is what we can then, in turn, share with others.

▶ TAKE ACTION ◀

- **Top of Mind.** The next time someone shares something painful, instead of auto-advice giving, listen, reflect, and validate. For example, you could say, "I can hear that you feel hurt. That must have been really hard." Ultimately, what we all really want is to be seen, heard, and understood.

- **Take Care.** Engage in gentle stretching or yoga. This can help release physical tension and promote relaxation. Focus on your body and breath as you move through each pose.

- **Go Deeper: Codependency vs. Healthy Dependency.** It's time to explore the differences between codependency and healthy dependency. Go to page 237 in the "Go Deeper" section at the back of the book to keep raising your awareness on this key issue.

CHAPTER 5

Why Narcissists and Codependents Attract

WHEN LEIA, a successful PR strategist in her late thirties, first came to see me, she was exhausted, confused, and determined to learn from a nightmarish relationship she'd recently ended. In explaining her reason for seeking treatment, she said, "I want to understand how I could have possibly fallen for someone like him."

From that statement alone, I suspected that Leia was being unnecessarily hard on herself. She was not the first highly capable woman to be taken in by a toxic person.

"Let's start from the beginning," I said. "How did you meet this person?"

Leia explained that, on a whim, she invited Andy, an acquaintance at the time, to a party she was hosting. Andy had brought an extravagant gift, so afterward she called to thank him and suggested they have dinner. To Leia, this was a collegial get-together, but Andy was clearly interested in being more than friends.

At dinner, Leia was pleasantly surprised to discover they had a lot in common. He, too, was an introvert. They shared the same taste in books and movies. In Andy, she felt like she'd found a good friend.

For most of Leia's life, she felt like an outsider. Born and raised in Asia, she moved stateside as a teenager and had a hard time fitting in. Leia was studious and found solace in her classes, becoming interested in feminist and women's studies. Starting her own business and helping other female entrepreneurs had gone a long way in helping Leia find her voice and her community. But when Leia met Andy, she felt a strong kinship that spoke to the hidden part of her that still yearned for belonging.

After months of Andy proving himself a trustworthy friend, Leia started to wonder if they could be more.

Andy showered her with compliments, affection, and gifts. Eventually, she gave in and found herself head over heels in love. The more time they spent together as a couple, the more certain Leia was that she'd been waiting for Andy her whole life.

Yet even amid Andy's charm offensive, there were a few things that Leia thought were odd, like the fact that he had no friends or social circle and was jealous of her past romances and male colleagues. Leia rationalized this behavior away. If she'd been waiting for this guy her whole life, what were a few hiccups?

A few months in, Andy had inserted himself in every aspect of her business, from interviewing new prospective hires to making decisions about the advertising budget. He also suggested that none of Leia's employees had her back, unlike him. He was meticulously sowing doubt in her as her paranoia ballooned. From there, Andy moved on to criticizing how she ran her business. He always couched his criticisms in terms of his love and concern for Leia. For her part, she really wanted to believe him.

Andy eventually convinced Leia to scale down her team and put him in charge of operations and finance. Leia put all her trust in him.

In their personal relationship, he began sending mixed signals, too, telling Leia she needed a night off and then disparaging her when she took his advice, saying things like, "You're so checked out and you don't even care how hard I'm working for your business."

Leia made excuses for him, thinking, *He doesn't really mean what he's saying. I'll deal with this later, it's too hectic right now.* As Leia explained to me, "It's easy to make excuses for someone when you're in love."

Things went from bad to worse. Andy became brazen about his demands. For example, he woke her up on a Sunday by barking an order that she complete a spreadsheet ASAP. Somehow, he had taken over. She couldn't do anything right.

Miserable, Leia began opening up to a few trusted friends. She didn't want to be a burden or judged as "stupid" for being in this toxic relationship. But getting real with her pals was a critical step. It made it easier for Leia to admit that there was nothing remotely okay about this relationship. Shortly after telling the truth to her friends, she started to seriously consider leaving him.

Sensing that Leia was cooling off, Andy went into "good guy" mode. He started therapy and confided in her about being abused as a child. When he made overwrought pleas for her to believe in his ability to change, Leia took the bait—so much so that she agreed to move with him out of state, away from friends and a support network.

Within a week of moving, Andy reverted to moodiness, hostility, and belittling her feelings. He even told her that their couple's therapist thought she was the problem (which wasn't true). Their arguments escalated. Leia knew that the relationship couldn't be salvaged, but having taken several hits to her self-esteem, she felt stuck.

It wasn't until he picked a vicious fight over the contents of her private text messages—which he had no business reading—that she realized she had to get out immediately and stay out. Though he had never been physically abusive, his emotional and psychological violations were so extreme that Leia now felt she was in danger.

Shaking, Leia packed her bags and left. On the plane, she fully removed his access to all of her business accounts. She was *done*.

By the time Leia came to see me, she had been split from Andy for a few months. Initially, she'd leapt back into work, a safe space now that her toxic boyfriend was no longer involved. But she realized that she had some major healing to do—beginning with understanding how she came to be so vulnerable to an abuser like Andy.

Based on Leia's story, I had some thoughts—namely, their relationship had all the hallmarks of a narcissist-codependent dynamic. For Leia, who presented as an overachieving, *I-got-it* HFC, seeing the underpinnings of their relationship was pivotal in her healing journey.

The Narcissist/Codependent Attraction

The connection between codependents and narcissists is so prevalent and pernicious that it merits serious unpacking. Have you ever found yourself in a relationship with someone with strong narcissistic tendencies and traits, whether a lover, parent, sibling, or friend? The answer for many of us is *yes*. So why is this particular pairing so compelling? It is a seemingly perfect fit because narcissists and codependents comprise two halves of a perfectly dysfunctional relationship whole. You have the narcissist who's the self-focused taker and controller, and the codependent who's the other-focused giver and fixer. Both parties are mesmerized by the dance because unresolved childhood injuries are being played out, so it feels familiar.

This irresistible attraction leads to dysfunctional and disastrous results—a toxic cycle of behavior and psychological abuse that can go on for a lifetime unless there is some kind of shift in awareness or a pattern interruption. Being a high-functioning codependent adds an additional layer of glue to this already sticky dynamic. Our determination to fix and save can reach stratospheric levels. HFCs tend to give their relationships their all for way longer than makes sense.

> ### *Loving Reminder*
> Narcissists are selfish and self-centered and they are magnetized
> to the giving, self-sacrificing nature of the codependent.

If you've found yourself in a long-standing challenging relationship with a narc, the following may sound familiar:

If I can just find the perfect words to express myself . . . then he'll be able to hear me and want to change.

If I can just pick the right time to ask her this favor . . . then she'll show up for me like I do for her.

If I can just be more loving . . . then they'll stop being so critical and everything will be good again.

If you've been engaging in this kind of if/then reasoning for a while and are continually met with blame, anger, and manipulation, some part of you knows that this strategy is not going to move the needle one bit. In other words, if you're constantly self-abandoning to serve another person's black hole of need, it'll never be okay. Often, HFCs reach a breaking point when the pain becomes too great to ignore, as it had for Leia.

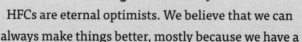

Loving Reminder 🖤
HFCs are eternal optimists. We believe that we can
always make things better, mostly because we have a
hard time accepting painful realities as they are.

Covert vs. Overt Narcissism

When you think about a narcissist, what comes to mind? Do you think of the life of the party bragging about their accomplishments to anyone who will listen? Or someone out there seducing people with their considerable charms only to torture them once they are caught in their narc web? This is called *overt narcissism*. It's recognizable and in plain sight.

But that's only part of the story. A lesser-known form of narcissism is *covert narcissism*, also known as *vulnerable narcissism*. The covert or vulnerable narc has a lot in common with overt narcs, though they are harder to spot because they're not out there bragging up a storm and hogging the proverbial mic. The following chart outlines the major differences between overt and covert narcs, as well as their commonalities:

THE COVERT NARCISSIST	BOTH	THE OVERT NARCISSIST
Shy, withdrawn, socially awkward.	Are incapable of empathy for others.	Charming, personable, outgoing.
Quietly superior. Thinks they deserve unlimited power, success, and adoration, but won't talk about it directly.	Have an inflated sense of their own importance.	Vocal about how they are better than everyone else and deserve more.
Needs constant reassurance and will put themselves down in order to get it.	Have a deep need for attention and admiration.	Does anything to draw attention to themselves. Will brag and exaggerate their accomplishments.

THE COVERT NARCISSIST	BOTH	THE OVERT NARCISSIST
Passive-aggressive in communication and behaviors.	Feed off the emotional pain of others.	Directly aggressive and toxic in their behavior and communication.
Gets extremely defensive and constantly feels criticized.	Are thin-skinned and sensitive to criticism.	Outwardly and vocally flip out over any perceived slight.
Jealous of others and will make passive-aggressive comments like, "Must be nice to get so many lucky breaks in life . . ."	Have troubled and toxic relationships.	Directly puts others down.
Will quietly bide their time until they can exact revenge.	Hold grudges.	Vocal about who did them wrong and the revenge they will take.
Tends toward anxiety and depression.	Have secret feelings of insecurity and shame.	Tends toward rage and contempt.
Has a "life is unfair" attitude and victim mentality.	Take advantage of others to get what they want.	Expects preferential treatment from others.
Extra skilled at faking empathy.	Believe they deserve what others have.	Feels and acts entitled to "the best" of everything.

→ CHECK IN

Bring to mind several of your most difficult relationships—romantic, familial, or work-related. If you suspect narcissism is present, how does knowing about the types of narcissism influence your understanding of these people or your interactions with them?

It can be pretty terrifying to wake up one day and realize that the person you fell in love with, or befriended, or who raised you is a narcissist. It's shocking to admit that they do not actually have the capacity to understand or respect your feelings, and, in fact, have been subjecting you to subtle digs, undermining behaviors, and overall toxic ways. Covert narcissists are especially dangerous because they're heavily invested in concealing their self-absorbed, superior-than-thou nature, and are generally very good at cloaking their true intentions. When you don't know who you're dealing with, you're likely to let your guard down and become vulnerable to someone who may later use your vulnerability or whatever you've shared in confidence against you.

If you suspect that a close loved one falls into either category of overt or covert narcissism, don't worry if others think they're great. Big picture, it doesn't really matter if anyone agrees with you. What matters first and foremost is that you believe yourself. Especially with covert narcs, you might even choose to keep your assessments to yourself, rather than get caught up in having to prove why someone is emotionally unsafe for you to be around.

Say It with Me 💬

I respect, honor, and embrace my sensitivities. I know that with healthy self-care and consideration, they are my superpowers.

How We Got Here:
The Impact of Narcissistic Parents

When it comes to dysfunctional families, it doesn't get more crazy-making than the narcissistic family system. Children of narcs are conditioned from their earliest development to tend to their parent's needs, which negatively impacts their own development and can remain a painful and isolating experience into adulthood. And you don't have to have had a narc parent to fall prey to the toxic narc-codependent dance. There are many reasons you may be susceptible, including struggling with low self-esteem, self-worth, being a highly sensitive person or empath, and/or experiencing instability in your childhood home. Narcs are experts at exploiting weakness and a less-than-solid sense of self. However, if you did grow up with a parent or caregiver who was narcissistic, you are even more at-risk for winding up in relationships with narcissistic types. Learning to identify these behaviors and traits and validate yourself is of the utmost importance.

Daughters of Narcissistic Mothers

Being the daughter of a narc mother is especially damaging to your self-esteem and sense of self. As developing little humans, we need our mothers to help us learn about our emotions and manage them. When kids are upset, it's often the mom who notices and takes action to make the child feel seen, heard, and validated. If your mom had narc traits that likely did not happen. Daughters of narc mothers grow up feeling like nothing they do is good enough—like they are not enough. This can take a wrecking ball to the development of healthy self-esteem and not only lead to dysfunctional relational patterns in adulthood, but also extreme levels of self-doubt, self-criticism, and perfectionism. It can also be a catalyst for eating disorders, depression, disordered boundaries, difficult relationships, and fears of intimacy. Many daughters of narcissistic mothers even opt out of motherhood, due to fears of repeating the painful cycle with a daughter of their own.

When it comes to sharing your life with a narc mom, nothing you ever do or feel will be treated as important or special. Your wedding, promotion, and children will wind up somehow being about her, leaving you out in the cold. When you call her out, she'll resort to terrorist-grade guilt trips and outright lies, denying that she's said and done things you witnessed firsthand. A common card the narc mom plays: "I can't believe you would treat me this way. You'll be sorry when I'm dead." The narc mom is quick to deflect and blame her behavior on others or justify it by saying, "I'm your mother," as if the fact that she gave birth to you entitles her to total and complete access to your life, to infinity and beyond.

Having a narcissistic mom can create a deep sense of emptiness and loneliness. You may attempt to avoid this emotional pain by being in the perpetual motion of *doing too much*, never stopping to let yourself *be* or *feel*. Part of what makes this experience so isolating is that our society reveres mothers. So, if you didn't have a mother who fit the cookie-baking, nurturing-superhero, always-giving mother mold, you probably have no desire to share your genuine experiences. Growing up with a maternal narcissist is often a dirty secret. We're expected to put moms on pedestals, but if your mom was self-focused, negligent, and emotionally manipulative, it can be hard to pretend.

Folks with healthier moms might inadvertently compound the pain by saying thoughtless things like, "Well, *all* mothers can be annoying," or, "All mothers deserve respect." It's like, okay, but do *all* mothers psychologically abuse their children and scar them for life?

I'm giving an extra shout-out to the daughters of narcissistic mothers because this experience is so uniquely excruciating that I want you to know that you are seen and you are loved simply for being who you are. No matter how you decide to deal with your mother as an adult (low-contact, no-contact, bitter obligation, or edgy humor) the choice is yours, no matter what others think.

BACK TO YOU
The Narc Family System

Each member in a narc family system has a role that helps keep the dysfunction rolling along. These are assigned and carried out unconsciously but have a powerful—and powerfully damaging—effect. The roles include:

- The golden child, whose job is to make the family look good.

- The scapegoat, whose job is to act out the veiled feelings of the group.

- The flying monkey, whose job is to carry out the needs and wants of the narc.

- The enabler, whose job is to sacrifice themselves to support the narc's beliefs.

Do you identify yourself, your siblings, or other family members in any of these roles?

DARVO

Narcissistic family systems subject all members to the judo-level mind games of the narc. When confronted with their double standards, unacceptable behavior, and/or abuse, narcs are skilled at DARVO. This acronym explains the narc's favorite defense tactic—deny the behavior, attack the person who is bringing the bad behavior to light, reverse the roles of victim and offender. DARVO was coined by Dr. Jennifer Freyd, coauthor (with Pamela Birrell) of *Blind to Betrayal: Why We Fool Ourselves We Aren't Being Fooled* and born out of Freyd's horrifying life experience. Betrayal blindness means not seeing what is right in front of us and instead blaming the person who is being abused.

In her early thirties, Freyd suddenly recalled a familial betrayal that had been there all along—being molested by her father. Though she had no plans of going public or even sharing beyond her close circle of loved ones, her parents went into full-blown attack mode when they learned of her memories resurfacing. They established the False Memory Syndrome Foundation in an effort to discredit her (and, subsequently, countless other abuse victims). Her mother wrote for a journal an anonymous article about false allegations, in which she cast aspersions on her daughter's character. Her mother sent this article to Freyd's colleagues, and in some cases, included a personal note signed with her name, making Freyd's identity crystal clear. There's no world in which a healthy, or caring parent vilifies their child in this way. If what Freyd was saying was false, any normal parent would have sought to help her, not violate and attack her.

Freyd's experience is an extreme illustration of DARVO, but you may have witnessed similar iterations in your own life. Classic examples of DARVO include the cheating spouse who accuses his wife of being unfaithful, or the parent who denies making cruel digs and instead tries to place the blame on the child he's wronged. In each case, the perpetrator casts him- or herself as the helpless victim. DARVO creates a smokescreen that can be hard to see beyond and thus has a chilling effect on truth telling. It's the narcissist's highly effective defense against anyone who dares to name real transgressions. It's often easier to remain blind to betrayals in personal relationships with a narcissist. If this experience resonates, please know that you're not alone and your blindness to betrayal has served the purpose of basic safety and survival.

In reality, every member in the narcissistic family system is victimized in some way because the family system is rife with pain and tragedy. If this speaks to your experience and you have challenging relationships with your siblings, then you know exactly what I'm talking about. Everyone was just trying to make it out of that horror show alive.

Regardless of what anyone else thinks, if you were raised by a narc, it's important to get real about what was not okay about your upbringing. Once we recognize unhealthy patterning, we can start to make different choices. Our parents may not change, but we can stop the cycle in our own lives.

- **It was not okay to be emotionally blackmailed and guilt-tripped.**

- **It was not okay to have your feelings belittled and ridiculed.**

- **It was not okay for your parents to triangulate you with your siblings.**

- **It was not okay for them to withdraw love and attention if you didn't do exactly what they wanted.**

- **It was not okay for them to be jealous of things you felt good about.**

If any of the points above are relatable, your family may have had narcissistic personalities in it. Any form of narcissistic abuse is not okay—and the kid in you needs to know you understand this and have her back. Honestly honoring your childhood experiences is an important aspect of healing.

> ### *Say It with Me* 💬
> I love, honor, respect, and protect my
> inner child. Now and always.

Life After Being Raised by Narcs

In your present-day life, you might see the impact of growing up under the tyranny of a narcissistic parent in a number of ways, from the compulsion to over-extend yourself to having disordered boundaries. For example, exercising the right to like (and not like) whatever you so choose—children of narcs struggle to establish their own autonomy and personal rules of engagement. They question their right to protect themselves and are plagued with self-doubt and a lack of self-trust. It's hard to identify what taking care of themselves actually entails. Narcissists are what I call "boundary destroyers"—meaning they do not respect and honor another person's preferences, feelings, or boundaries—so, if you're a child of a narc, you may still be fearful of speaking your mind and letting others know what is and isn't okay with you. In childhood, if you were stuck with an abusive parent, you had no choice but to go along with their rules. But in adulthood, the lingering effects of your compliance become extremely problematic as you attempt to exercise any personal agency. You may find yourself saying yes to crap you do not want to be saying yes to or holding back your true feelings in order to avoid even a hint of conflict.

BACK TO YOU
Boundary Boss Bill of Rights

In my therapy practice, many of my clients struggle to identify their relationship rights. This struggle is even more intense if they have been in toxic or challenging relationships. The Boundary Boss Bill of Rights below is from my book, *Boundary Boss*. You can use it as a guide when you are feeling unsure of your relationship rights.

◻ I have the right to say no (or yes) to others without feeling guilty.

◻ I have the right to make mistakes, course correct, or change my mind.

◻ I have the right to negotiate for my preferences, desires, and needs.

◻ I have the right to express and honor all my feelings if I so choose.

◻ I have the right to voice my opinion even if others disagree.

◻ I have the right to be treated with respect, consideration, and care.

◻ I have the right to determine who has the privilege of being in my life.

◻ I have the right to communicate my boundaries, limits, and deal-breakers.

◻ I have the right to prioritize my self-care without feeling selfish.

◻ I have the right to talk true, be seen, and live free.

Reflect on these rights, affirm them daily, and let them be your guiding principles. As you speak each one aloud, look into the mirror to reaffirm the person you are reclaiming and the new relational patterns you are setting. This practice is not just about recovery; it's about empowerment.

The more we explored Leia's early life conditioning, the more she understood that her childhood experiences primed her for her abusive relationship with Andy.

Growing up, Leia was always on edge, very aware that to gain any form of praise or love, she needed to be seen as exceptional, not in her own right, but as her father's daughter. Though she experienced relief as a teenager at boarding school, she never fully recognized the ways that her father's insistence that her life be *all about him* had affected her self-identity and self-worth. She covered up her insecurities by being studious and smart and becoming very successful. No question, her achievements felt good to her, but without looking back to her childhood to heal those inner wounds, she was definitely at risk for falling for someone like Andy, whose narcissism fit her codependency like a glove. At points during their relationship, she had flashes of awareness—*Why am I afraid of being punished? Why is this feeling so familiar?* But her awareness never reached full bloom, in part because she was constantly in survival mode, trying to make Andy happy so they could go back to "the way they were." In reality, the happy beginning was a myth and therefore unrecoverable.

In one breakthrough session Leia declared out loud, "Whoa, that relationship was horrible, I really dodged a bullet." And she had, mostly because she had the good sense to finally confide in her close friends the truth about what was really happening.

I cannot underscore enough the importance of disclosing toxicity. This is hard for anyone indoctrinated in the narc family's loyalty code. In narcissistic family systems, loyalty isn't free-flowing or reciprocated *at all*. Everyone is expected to keep secrets and ignore terrible behavior in the name of protecting the family's reputation. Dr. Ramani Durvasula, psychologist and author of *It's Not You: Identifying and Healing from Narcissistic People*, asks a pointed question about loyalty in one of her YouTube videos: "At what point is loyalty on a one-way street to self-harm?" Doctor Ramani, as she's known on YouTube, underscores the inherent damage to those who genuinely pride themselves on being loyal, only to have that become an obstacle to naming what is obviously abusive behavior in the context of a narc family system. The choice is to endure gaslighting, manipulation, and abuse *or* risk being criticized by those in the family system who call the truth-teller disloyal. "Loyalty," she points out, "is not meant to be masochism. Loyalty is not meant to be 'stand around and be taken advantage of.'"

Inner courage is required when you dare to step outside the confining box of narc families and relationships and start to admit the truth of what you're living through or have lived through. Make your healing more important than the threat of being criticized, judged, or cast out by folks who really haven't earned your respect, much less an outsized influence over your healing process.

For Leia, breaking rank came when she stopped blaming herself, and started taking a stand for herself and her healing.

Loving Reminder 🖤
Speaking to a trusted friend or therapist about a challenging relationship can be a powerful step toward healing.

Avoiding Future Narc Relationships

Once you're in a place of physical and emotional safety, healing from this tough dynamic can start, as Leia discovered. Leia's personal power increased exponentially within months of starting therapy. Feelings she'd avoided by overworking and getting caught up in the drama with Andy came back in full force—and processing those feelings was profoundly helpful to reclaiming her life.

For people who finally get out of a narc relationship, there is a deep fear of repeating it. Doing an inventory of the red flags they missed in the early days of close relationships with narcissists can be a super valuable exercise in understanding what happened and what behaviors to be on guard for in the future. That was definitely the case for Leia. She hadn't completely missed the red flags—for example she found it odd Andy didn't have close friends and felt a physical pang of discomfort when he made controlling moves to isolate her from her colleagues and community. When we can name them in hindsight, that means some part of us was aware of the other person's bad behavior. This is not an invitation to beat yourself up, as in, *How did I let that happen?* A better reframe is, *How can I take an honest inventory of what was happening for me that I ignored the red flags?*

BACK TO YOU
Red and Green Relationship Flags

One of the easiest ways to avoid getting into a relationship with a narcissist is to be aware of behavioral red and green flags. Use the list below to identify healthy and unhealthy behaviors.

How many items on the red flag list have you experienced? Which items on the green flag list do you want more of in your relationships? Take a moment to journal your answers.

RED FLAGS	GREEN FLAGS
• Avoids being vulnerable (and asks you many personal questions so that *you* will be vulnerable)	• Can be appropriately vulnerable
• Lacks empathy	• Has empathy for themselves and others
• Feels entitled to special treatment	• Expects appropriate consideration
• Needs to be the center of attention	• Can share and listen in conversation
• Doesn't keep their word	• Reliable and keeps their word
• Can be manipulative	• Direct about their desires and intentions
• Is arrogant	• Has good self-esteem and humility
• Treats people "below" them badly	• Treats all people with respect
• Blames others for their mistakes	• Takes responsibility for their actions
• Believes they are exceptional	• Appropriately transparent
• Overly secretive	• Truthful
• Exploits others	• Consistently treats you with kindness
• Gaslights, denying your reality	• Talks about actual accomplishments and things they are proud of
• Love bombs; overly loving and complimentary in the beginning	• Clear, concise, and consistent communication
• Talks about fantasies of success and power	• Good listener
• Is envious of others	• Makes others feel safe
• Inconsistent communication	
• Bad listener	
• Makes others feel insecure	

As Leia sifted through the mountain of red flags Andy had exhibited, she began to feel calmer. She could see how her eagerness to connect and feel less alone, coupled with her people-pleasing nature, had been contributing factors to her overriding uneasiness at various points throughout their relationship. Understanding how she'd self-abandoned was vital to her healing.

Andy periodically tried to contact her, but she was well on her healing journey. With the support of her close friends, she was able to successfully cut off all contact for good. Self-care and boundaries were an integral part of the breaking away process for Leia, and they continue to be important in healing and living going forward.

If you have experienced this kind of psychological and emotional abuse, give yourself time to heal. We don't get over these kinds of toxic relationships in any specific timeframe, but we can learn to grow through the pain and heartbreak by consciously developing our trust in ourselves and validating our emotional experiences.

Say It with Me 💬
I forgive myself with ease, sincerity, and loving compassion.

Leia's life looks dramatically different than when she first walked into my therapy office several years ago. After a sustained effort to care for herself that included nature walks and spending time with trusted friends, she became passionate about sharing her story to raise awareness around the seriousness of emotional abuse. She wanted to let other women know that they're not alone and they don't need to take all the blame for being taken in by a master manipulator. The biggest obstacle for Leia was learning to make peace with herself, via self-forgiveness, which is deep and meaningful work and an ongoing process. From all her hard work, Leia has reclaimed her power and joy.

And I have no doubt that no matter what your life experience, you absolutely can, too. Trust yourself, the universe, and the healing process.

▶ TAKE ACTION ◀

- **Top of Mind.** If you have any big decisions to make this week, sit someplace quiet, take a few deep, grounding breaths, bring the decision to mind, and pay attention to how your body reacts. The more you dial into your body, the more access you will have to your gut instincts and intuition.

- **Take Care.** Treat yourself to a warm bath or shower with soothing elements like scented candles, essential oils, or calming music. Creating a spa-like atmosphere is a simple but effective way to relax and rejuvenate.

- **Go Deeper: Understanding Love Bombing.** Let's dig into how narcissists hook their prey. Go to page 241 in the "Go Deeper" section at the back of the book to learn more about the narcissist abuse cycle and the tactics they use to disarm and control.

CHAPTER 6

The High Cost of Being HFC

ERIKA WAS A late forty-something business exec who came to me during a particularly stressful time in her long, successful career. A corporate merger had turned her seventy-hour workweek to ninety. At her wit's end, Erika had developed symptoms of burnout that were affecting her ability to function. She came to me in the hope that we could crack the energy code, so that she could finally feel calm and rested enough to keep up with her insane schedule.

Even though she had little time to even think, let alone take care of herself, she was fully prepared to power through and keep over-functioning, exhaustion and chronic stress be damned. Work and managing her staff through the merger dominated ninety-nine percent of her thoughts.

In our sessions, she kept hoping the dust would settle soon. Then one day, she walked in shaking her head.

"You are not going to believe this!" she said. "I was laid off today."

"I'm so sorry," I replied. "What happened?"

Erika explained that her bosses were hiring a younger woman with less experience to take her place.

"They said it was due to budget cuts. They said it was 'just business,'" Erika said, fuming. Yet it clearly felt personal to her.

"Was it 'just business' when I personally counseled my boss' son after one of their horrific fights and helped them mend fences? Not exactly 'just business' when I invested in his sister's baking company, even though her cookies tasted like sawdust!"

Years of suppressed resentment came spilling out as she listed all the sacrifices she'd made for her bosses and colleagues over the past fifteen years.

"I've done all the right things, Terri. Went to a good school. Worked my way up the corporate ladder. Showed up for basically *anyone* in need. I mean, seriously, what's it all for if my career and life can be blown up in a thirty-minute meeting?"

Hyperbole aside, this sudden professional rupture had an unexpected effect. It deeply challenged the idea that Erika had been living a fulfilled life. She had not.

"And now my youngest is off to college next year. Then my husband and I will be empty nesters and who knows if we even like each other anymore?" she lamented. "I think of what I missed with my boys when they were younger—and for what? To be a good soldier at work until they kicked me to the curb?"

Erika was realizing with shock the far-reaching effects of her HFC behaviors. They cost her precious time she couldn't get back with those she loved the most—her husband and kids. There was also the personal cost of not deeply knowing herself. She was so focused on work that she had little energy or desire for self-reflection.

"It sounds like you've spent a whole lot of time pouring your energy into others' happiness and well-being," I observed. "How would it feel if we focused on you right now?"

Erika's face went blank. "Me? Uh . . ."

I knew that this big shock was also a big opportunity for Erika to transform her HFC tendencies toward a more balanced and satisfying life.

Being HFC with the World

Often, HFCs are not just codependent with their inner circle of family and friends, they're also codependently concerned about everyone in the wider world as well, including acquaintances, coworkers, or in some cases, total strangers. It is as if they cannot turn off their empathy and are naturally drawn to people in need. This is especially true for extroverted empaths, like me.

Pre-recovery, when I behaved as if I were genuinely codependent with everybody and their mother, I had more than my fair share of absurd experiences. Case in point—in my twenties, I attended a weekend training to become a volunteer advocate for rape survivors, where I met Barb, a fellow twenty-something volunteer. Shortly after we met, Barb confessed that she was being physically and emotionally abused by her husband. My sense of urgency was immediately activated. I spent the rest of the day making a case for Barb to leave him.

One night soon after, Barb texted that she was in danger and asked if she could please come over. An hour later, she showed up at my 600-square foot studio apartment with her dog and six bags. "I did it," she said. "Thanks to your encouragement, I left him."

"That's . . . great, Barb," I said, as I eyed her bags nervously. Was that a winter coat I spied—in July? How long was she planning on staying?

"Can I just stay with you for like a few days until I sort out where to go next?"

"Uh . . . sure," I said, feeling trapped.

I didn't actually want Barb and Sunshine, her hyperactive Frenchie, sharing my full-sized bed or any corner of my tiny apartment. Yet, despite barely knowing this woman, I felt responsible for her safety. And that's what kept me from saying anything as a few days bled into a week.

To Barb's face, I smiled and acted like things were cool. Out of earshot, I was frantically calling friends. The response I received was universal: "Are you freaking nuts, Ter?"

I wasn't nuts, I just felt overly responsible for a fellow human in need. Like my reaction to Billy, the kid on the train platform in New

York City, and my sister Jenna, there was no self-reflection, just react-ing to make it "right." Having to be at the heart of so many people's solutions regardless of how (or if!) I knew them was exhausting and unnecessary. At the time, I did not know I could be supportive with-out fully taking on Barb's situation.

On day seven of Barb's stay, my landlord spotted her and Sunshine in the hallway. I said she was my cousin who was just staying for a few days. He swiftly reminded me I was in breach of my lease agreement that clearly stated, "no dogs allowed," and gave Barb and Sunshine twenty-four hours to vacate. Her cousin from Albany came to pick her up the next day. Phew!

For Erika, over-working and over-giving to her boss' family mem-bers in order to be liked and to be seen as indispensable worked for a while. But the cost was her health, her family, and her happiness—sacrifices that ultimately did not save her job, either.

Self-Abandonment and "Peace at Any Price"

HFCs abandon themselves so fast and so well that they hardly even notice that they have their own needs, wants, or preferences. Self-abandonment is when we reject, suppress, or ignore parts of ourselves. It is when we are out of tune with our own preferences, needs, and wants. Usually, this accompanies being super dialed into everyone else. It can sound like, "It's fine, no problem, you take the car, and I'll just get an Uber," or, "Sure, come live with me for an unspecified amount of time," or, "No problem, I can stay late again at work tonight so you can attend your kid's volleyball game." It can show up in big or small ways at home, at work, and in our day-to-day lives. Its impact is cumulative. For Erika, regularly miss-ing family events, not scheduling time to exercise or see friends, and working on weekends (so when she *was* home she wasn't really there), all took their toll and eventually led her to burn out.

Even though there is a tendency to categorize an array of experiences as *fine*, in reality, self-abandonment is not "fine"—not in the moment and not over the long-term. Inconveniencing yourself to serve the greater good is appropriate and makes sense at times, but habitually overriding what you want, need, and desire to make others happy (or just *not* annoyed or angry) will breed chronic resentment, as we explored in chapter 1.

Many HFCs operate under the guiding principle of "peace at any price." It helps us get through uncomfortable situations. It might look like always hosting family holidays, even if it leaves you bone tired, simply because you don't want to upset anyone by suggesting a change. Or this could involve always letting your partner choose the movie, restaurant, or vacation spot because you'd rather sacrifice your preferences than risk an argument. But "peace at any price" is not realistic, especially if you're the only one paying the price. Sooner or later, you will erupt if you've been treating yourself like your needs don't matter.

The biggest things we lose by clinging to our (unconscious) motto of "peace at any price," are being seen for who we are; having authentic, mutually reciprocal relationships; experiencing genuine inner peace; and having precious time and energy to do what we came to Earth School to do. These are important experiences that give our lives meaning. We don't want to miss them.

Determined to live differently, Erika began to look at life through her own eyes, not the lens of what others needed, thought, or had grown to expect.

BACK TO YOU
Are You Self-Abandoning?

Below are some common signs you might be self-abandoning. See yourself in any?

☐ You rarely set or keep boundaries.

☐ You frequently second-guess yourself.

☐ You identify as a people pleaser.

☐ You suffer from perfectionism.

☐ You have a loud and mean "inner critic."

☐ Your self-care barely exists.

☐ You engage in self-numbing behavior.

If you recognize yourself in any of these examples of self-abandonment, rest assured you are not alone. You now know there is work to be done.

How We Cope

Coming face-to-face with the personal price Erika had paid as an HFC—quality time with her sons and husband, her unlived dreams, way, *way* too much work (and NOT ENOUGH sleep)—was sobering and eye-opening. But even so, in our weekly sessions, Erika admitted that she was still being pulled back in the direction of codependency. One of her former coworkers called her in tears, and so she skipped yoga to counsel this young woman for two hours. She continued to regularly give career (and life) advice to her old assistant who was looking for a new job, too, and somehow got roped into fostering her neighbor's dog for a month. Erika did not honestly want to do any of those things. In session she said, "It happens so quick. How do I stop?"

Secondary Gain

For Erika to move forward, we had to reveal what she gained from staying stuck in these unhealthy behaviors. It sounds counterintuitive, but anyone stuck in repeated negative behaviors, situations, or relationships receives some kind of Secondary Gain, or a psychological pay-off. There is a nonobvious benefit from repeating these behaviors that we're saying we don't want. With primary gain, the benefit is obvious: if you are ambitious and spend most of your time working, you will advance in your career. But with Secondary Gain, the benefit operates below our conscious awareness. By regularly staying late at work, you may also get to avoid facing an unhappy domestic situation. So, identifying Secondary Gain increases our self-knowledge and gives us a better chance at resolving our resistance and enacting the changes we're wanting to consciously make.

> ### Loving Reminder 🖤
> Understanding yourself more deeply becomes the catalyst
> to stop self-sabotaging behaviors. This frees you to create
> healthier relationships with yourself and others.

When you ask yourself, "What is the nonobvious benefit of this undesirable situation I often find myself in?" you may be surprised how fast the answer comes. For example, during the early days of the pandemic, a client was desperate to quit alcohol, but like so many folks during that unprecedented time in global history, she was drinking like a fish. After a few weeks of her cycling through the stop-start of margarita consumption, I asked her, "What do you get to avoid by nightly drinking?" Her answer came tumbling right out: "That my marriage is over." That's the power of Secondary Gain.

My Secondary Gain for staying in the savior position with my sister Jenna was not having to experience my feelings of extreme helplessness, or face disappointing my mother who I felt was depending on me to get it handled (she was "the fixer" in her family of origin, too). As long as I was plotting and planning ways to save my sister, I could avoid my pain and continue to deny the truth that her situation was not mine to manage. As Bev helped me see (chapter 2), it was beyond my control. I could not actually "fix" anything.

For Erika, her Secondary Gain became clear. By busying herself with other people's problems, she got to avoid feeling inadequate, bringing back old, painful feelings from her childhood. Neither of her parents were tuned in to her emotionally, which wrecked Erika's self-esteem. Her dad liked his martini nights. Her mom was hyperfocused on keeping the house spotless. As a result, Erika grew up feeling unseen. The one time Erika had excitedly come home from music class and declared she wanted to become a singer, her mother just rolled her eyes and kept scrubbing the kitchen sink. Her parents' emotional neglect had left a lasting mark. To gain some semblance of emotional connection, Erika learned to make herself indispensable to *others*. In adulthood, her self-abandonment was painful and costly, but it also protected her from feeling the emotional barrenness of her early life. Erika admitted that the scared kid in her still felt pretty overwhelmed by sadness and fear that she wasn't good enough. It also kept her from revisiting her long-held desire, which was to learn to sing.

Pain is the single greatest motivator to change. So, if our Secondary Gain prevents us from feeling our pain, guess what? Our motivation to change disappears. We stay in the "known" and risk nothing.

We stay safe, but at some point or another, that worn out version of safety fails us, and we're stuck in a less than satisfying life.

→ CHECK IN

If you find yourself repeating unwanted relationships or situations, you can use the Secondary Gain tool below to reveal the unobvious gain for staying stuck, which will make it that much easier to get unstuck.

Ask yourself: *What do I get to not face, not feel, or not experience by staying stuck in this unwanted behavior pattern?*

Shadow Addictions

Secondary gain can be accompanied by *shadow addictions*, a term I coined to describe socially acceptable behaviors that numb our emotions and create distractions that keep us in familiar dysfunctional patterns and behaviors. These behaviors can include but are not limited to retail therapy, nightly alcohol or cannabis consumption, workaholism, overexercising, overeating, doom-scrolling, or Netflix binging. Whatever the form, they help us "relax" and anesthetize our pain, fears of rejection, vulnerability, or inadequacy.

Even though shadow addictions might not lead immediately (or ever) to the total shitshow that full-blown addictions tend to, they foster emotional confusion instead of emotional clarity, and that blocks our growth. Besides dulling the pain that could motivate us to personally evolve, these dysfunctional behaviors will eventually create distraction pain (like poor health or booze-fueled drama) that co-opt our bandwidth and drain our energy. There's not a whole lot of psychic space to be present in life when we're constantly putting out the fires we unconsciously set to distract ourselves from the real issues. *Wait . . . I'm the pyro??*

Shadow addictions do not necessarily interfere with managing your everyday life responsibilities, such as work, working out, or taking care of kids, but not being debilitated does not mean the behavior is not negatively impacting the quality of your life. Essentially, numbing your emotions is a way to rob yourself of the impetus to feel, deal, and heal. Shadow addictions fuel our resistance to change.

Recognizing that her inner child was still very scared and sad—and that adult Erika was numbing herself with nightly wine therapy—I invited Erika to consider spending time each night doing things she'd loved to do as a child. She was game.

This included singing, listening to music, getting creative with clay, drawing, coloring, and watching movies she used to love. Play had not been a part of Erika's experience for a very long time. The point was to spark creative and inspired feelings instead of numbing.

Numbing behaviors are short-term "solutions" to help us bypass our inner life. They are a way to avoid the uncomfortable feelings that arise from not being in control or not knowing how to interact authentically in our relationships. In contrast, soothing behaviors are healthy forms of relaxation or exertion, helping calm our nervous system and connect with ourselves. Examples of soothing behaviors are hiking, taking a yoga class, going for a walk with a pal, breathing exercises, and meditation. (In part 2 we cover soothing behaviors more in depth). For Erika, choosing to soothe through her nightly creativity sessions, along with long walks in the woods, helped immensely, allowing her to connect with her internal landscape, which helped her see life—and herself—more clearly.

What HFCs Miss Out On

As we covered in chapter 4, being HFC can prevent us from going to deeper levels with the folks who matter most to us. When we're quick to fix people's situations, we don't allow for normal human fallibility—in ourselves and others. We block ourselves from being vulnerable or receiving other people's real trust. This also keeps intimacy at bay, leading to a lack of fulfillment all around.

What we may not realize is that taking automatic, energetic responsibility for what's not ours—or doing *too much* to get it all *just right*—takes up precious resources we could be spending on our own lives, relationships, and pursuits. Energy leaks are seriously consequential for HFCs, especially those who are empaths or highly sensitive and who are on high alert 24/7 to what's going on with other people. As we've learned in earlier chapters, as an HFC, you may be leaking your energy everywhere by over-giving, over-functioning, people-pleasing, auto–advice giving, over-thinking, auto-accommodating, anticipatory planning, and perfectionism. You may not realize how much these behaviors are bleeding your energy dry.

Here is a brief list of some of the costs of chronic HFC behavior:

Quality Time with the Actual VIPs in Our Lives. When we say yes to lower-priority people we have less time, energy, and bandwidth for the actual VIPs in our lives. Only we can make the choice to carve out more time and space for the folks whose company is nourishing, fun, and inspirational, not the ones who drain us or perpetually bring us down.

Allowing Ourselves to Opt Out. Some of us can't even imagine what it would look or feel like to drop some of the balls we're juggling. So, we force ourselves to hit that early spin class or abandon our evening at home in the tub to come to the aid of a pal in need instead.

Spontaneity. Staying rigidly on course means we have little time to indulge our whims or say yes to spontaneous opportunities. Our need to control limits our ability to improvise and take advantage of whatever opportunities for unexpected adventure and joy arise.

When we look at how we've lost connection with ourselves, the cost is even more consequential. Here's what we may be missing out on:

Rest and Relaxation. For many of us, refueling our energy is super low on the priority list (if it's even a passing thought). Treating ourselves like machines is a surefire road to burnout.

Robust Health. For some, the cost of our HFC habits and compulsions on our well-being is monumental. We know that stress can lead to or exacerbate a myriad of health conditions, including heart issues, autoimmune diseases, and diabetes. The longer we've been stuck in the over-functioning mud, the greater the risk of developing a physical condition or compromising our mental health. We may physically or emotionally break down. Helper's fatigue (also known as compassion fatigue) can lead to mood swings and feeling drained overall.

Mental Alertness. Cognitive fatigue is another common HFC issue and the result of our brains overexerting on psychological, mental, and emotional levels. It's akin to running a marathon every day of the week without scheduling breaks. Self-care that includes good nutrition, regular movement, and a mindfulness practice can put us in a better position to enjoy optimal health. (In chapter 10 we'll cover more self-care ideas and strategies.)

A Healthy Relationship with Ourselves. Based on our early conditioning, we've learned to focus our time and attention outward. The hyper-attention on our environment (and the folks in it) means that our inner landscape is neglected. To become healthy, we can learn to put on our own oxygen mask first and foremost.

→ CHECK IN

As you scan through your HFC behaviors, notice where you may be feeling unfulfilled. Instead of over-functioning, how can you fill your own cup? What activities or downtime might help replenish your energy and optimism?

Exercising Choice

So, what does it look like to scrap compulsive and unconscious behaviors and instead give from conscious choice? Well, it means being present and engaged in every area of your life—without overpromising or doing more than your fair share. You fulfill your commitments, keep your word (to others and yourself), and stay mindful about what is and what is not your responsibility. Instead of staying hypervigilant about the desires of others, you can stay vigilant around your own well-being. Giving from love and choice provides you with the much-needed space to breathe, to respect your own limits, and to practice daily, consistent self-care.

An attitude of curiosity goes a long way as you continue to raise your self-awareness. One student made great (and quick) strides once she gave up her self-judgment and simply started looking at her life and behaviors anew through the HFC recovery lens. She was able to see how her need to be needed was interfering with pretty much every aspect of her life, including her work as a manicurist. Folks would sit in front of her and unload their innermost problems, fears, and dreams, and she'd immediately jump into *How can I help?* mode. She simply started asking herself questions, like, *Why do I do this? Is fixing problems for others how I derive my sense of self-worth and identity?* This process helped her slow down and create more space to explore her own desires. Now, she has an easier time listening to her clients with an open heart and mind, all curiosity and compassion, no need to fix or save. She leaves work feeling good and invigorated most days, with the energy to go to yoga or hiking with her dogs. Healthy giving and helping is a win-win for all involved.

> **Say It With Me** 💬
> It's okay for me to make mistakes, to course correct, or to change my mind.

The Grief That Comes with Growth

Once she fully realized the cost of her self-abandonment, Erika was priming herself to change her personal HFC game plan. Her wake-up call (getting fired) was bound to bring some buried or low-simmering resentment to the fore. Her resentment was fueled by the years, days, hours, minutes, and even seconds of ignoring her own needs—which would be enough to make anyone explode. As uncomfortable as this felt, I knew that if she got in touch with these feelings, it would serve her in the long-term. Erika became aware that if she didn't take her time to create a healthier relationship with her own needs, she could once again wind up burned out, spreading herself too thin, being overly focused on others, and feeling unfulfilled—something she did not want to fall back into as a soon-to-be empty nester. "It's almost like I have no choice but to focus on myself," she said.

As we evolve, we must mourn what will no longer be because of the changes we've made. In our sessions, Erika and I spent time processing her feelings of loss around missing pivotal experiences with her kids because of work. By honoring her real feelings, she was able to release her guilt and joyfully choose to prioritize her family relationships. As one of my HFC-in-recovery community members shared in a group session, "I find myself in a sea of change that shifted my perception so deeply that most everything in my life changed. My relationship with myself, my work, and the people in my life all underwent a huge transformation. It's all been so very good but there's also been some grief. I'm not the same person I was. I'm grateful I've become so confident and clear, but a part of my identity had to die to claim this healthier self."

As you continue on this journey, you may experience feelings of regret for the way you acted and interacted before becoming aware that you could do it differently. Honoring and processing significant losses, including relationships, careers, health, or your old self, is one way to make room for the satisfying life and relationships you're creating.

> ### Loving Reminder 🖤
> You are not meant to do it all alone. Ask, receive, allow.

Breaking the (Other) Glass Ceiling

You've probably heard of the glass ceiling—the invisible (yet extremely consequential) barrier that limits the professional advancement of marginalized and oppressed groups. Well, HFCs have a glass ceiling, too—a barrier to their personal and professional development and growth. Yet unlike the traditional glass ceiling, the HFC glass ceiling is one of our own making.

Think about it. When reactive behaviors and unconscious needs dictate how we spend our time and energy, there's only so far we can go in our life, and only so much success, fulfillment, connection, and adventure we can experience.

All of us have finite time and energy on this planet. When we learn to shift our autofocus away from others and toward our emotional, physical, and spiritual nourishment, we're not only healing lifelong HFC patterns, we're also opening ourselves to the inherent beauty of this precious and fleeting life. Some HFCs have devoted time and effort to incredible career achievements, while leaving their personal and emotional life on hold. However, if you're an HFC, you may not have had nearly enough bandwidth for developing your inner fulfillment or nurturing your most cherished dreams. There's some area of life where you are creating self-imposed limitations to what you can achieve and, more importantly, what you can feel, experience, and become in this lifetime.

Make shattering your own ceiling a top priority. You can learn to let go of the compulsive actions that don't serve you. Trust me, when you slow down and start hearing the drumbeat of your own soul, you are embarking on the grandest adventure of all. As you take back your personal agency, you'll remember the truly sacred nature of your sovereign being, your divine spark. You'll discover that there's a whole new world waiting for you.

> ### *Loving Reminder* 🖤
> Cultivating self-awareness helps you to recognize
> patterns and habits that may be holding you back. It lays
> the foundation for meaningful personal growth.

Eventually, Erika got up the courage to start taking singing lessons and soon dedicated her spare time to learning everything she could about breathing techniques and reading music. She marked off time in her calendar daily for this pursuit and added self-care to her schedule. It was part of her emotional hygiene and she committed to it as seriously as she would her physical hygiene. If she wouldn't miss a day of brushing her teeth, she wasn't going to miss a day of checking in with herself, either. Even when she only had ten minutes to meditate, that was enough to keep her rooted in her own experience.

Within a few months, Erika got a new job, which was stressful and fast-paced at times, but she never returned to full-blown HFC behaviors. She let her colleagues manage their own inner office conflicts and her bosses sort out their own family dynamics, leaving her to focus on the relationship that mattered most—the love affair she was beginning to have with herself. She kept up with her singing and told me she was trying to get up the courage to go to an open mic night at a local bar, something her husband was enthusiastically supporting. Pursuing singing as a hobby was an anchor of sorts, helping her weather inevitable transitions of becoming an empty nester, but it also served as an important reminder: *when we slow down and look inward, sustainable change is possible.*

▶ TAKE ACTION ◀

- **Top of Mind.** The next time you feel nervous, exhausted, or overwhelmed, notice how you respond. Do you numb your feelings with distractions or unhealthy habits? Or do you nurture yourself with self-care and compassion?

- **Take Care.** Practice deep, mindful breathing. Then before you start work, leave your house, or make a phone call, take slow, deliberate breaths and focus on the sensation of air filling your lungs and leaving your body. This can help calm your mind and center your thoughts.

- **Go Deeper: The Power Pivot.** We have to grieve the way things *were* to embrace how things *are*. This is true even when we experience changes we desire, like getting married, buying a home, or relocating for a dream job. Go to page 243 in the "Go Deeper" section at the back of the book for an exercise that can help you mourn any losses that need your attention.

PART 2

HFC in Recovery

Feeling, Allowing, and Doing Just Enough

CHAPTER 7

Becoming Emotionally Resilient

WHEN RANDI came to see me, she had a slew of admirable accomplishments under her belt. As a thirty-something domestic violence advocate, she was on the board of a DV shelter, worked tirelessly to change legislation, and counseled and championed women at some of the most pivotal and heart-wrenching moments of their lives. She was also a single mom to a young, spirited elementary-school-aged boy, who had an active sports schedule. Randi handled everything with passion and commitment. By all accounts, she was a badass.

Randi's work and son kept her busy and fired up. But in our first session she told me that as she approached her fourth decade of life, she was feeling dissatisfied. "My lack of a social life is starting to bother me. A friend suggested therapy might be a good place to start."

"If you had a social life," I asked, "what would that look like?"

Randi sighed and shook her head. "I really don't know. Just, like, not exclusively thinking about my work or kid."

Randi, I learned, was drawn to domestic violence work from personal experience. When she was nine years old, her father's psychological and emotional abuse had escalated to physical threats. Seizing an opportunity when he was out bowling, her mother scooped up Randi and her little sister, fleeing to a nearby shelter. As they bounced from one shelter to another, Randi encountered many children in similarly dire situations, which made a deep impression on her. Eventually, her mother won full custody and the three of them moved in with Randi's aunt. Though Randi's mother remarried a wonderful man and the rest of her childhood was relatively stable, that early life experience made a deep impression on her, and she grew up to do everything in her power to help the powerless.

Randi had a lot of fire and a huge heart, too. I could easily see how she persuaded people to donate money to shelters and moved lawmakers to act. She adopted her son after first being his foster mother when his birth mom died of a drug overdose. For all that she had been through and the level of heaviness that she encountered every day at work, Randi had a steady optimistic outlook on life. No matter how busy she was, if someone was in need, she spared no effort to help them: anyone, anytime, day or night.

"Wow," I said when she described helping a young single mom who called her in distress at 3:00 am in need of emergency housing. "That's a lot."

"It's just what I do," she said confidently.

Randi clearly had a higher calling. But at the same time, her HFC-ness was as strong as her convictions. As an advocate, she viewed responding to pleas for help as an integral part of her work, no matter when it was, or how big the request. She couldn't *not* help.

"How did hearing her plight make you feel?" I asked, hoping to gain insight into her state of mind.

"Well, she had a six-month-old baby, so it was critical to get them to safety."

In Randi's voice, I heard urgency and clarity about needing to act, but nothing about how Randi actually felt. It was similar to the way she told the story of being in the shelters as a kid: all the details were about her mother's fear, and nothing was about her own. Like many HFCs, Randi seemed disconnected from her own emotions. To reach greater levels of fulfillment, she would need to turn inward and get to know herself in a real way—perhaps for the first time.

As we've established, HFCs can tend toward being bighearted, highly sensitive, and empathic so the concept of being out of touch with their feelings may not make sense at first. You may be thinking, *But I feel all the time!* Yes, but much of the time it's *other people's* feelings that are dominating our internal experiences.

For example, asking an HFC how they are doing might inspire a cursory response ("I'm good!") before they launch into their thoughts about another person. They're worried/happy/sad about so-and-so, who just went into the hospital / received a raise / lost their beloved dog.

Many HFCs become experts on the feeling states of others—which is not the same as being emotionally intimate and comfortable with *themselves*—simply because they don't know how.

Learning to look within ourselves and acknowledge the range of real emotions that exist there builds emotional fluency and resilience. This internal resilience opens the door to new possibilities, empowering us to transform our relationship with ourselves and others.

Loving Reminder 🖤
Becoming emotionally resilient means learning to
slow down, feel your own feelings, and process them
without defaulting to reactivity or HFC behaviors.

Blocks to Turning Inward

Why do we find it so hard to be emotionally present?

One reason may surprise you: anticipatory anxiety. This is similar to anticipatory planning that we covered on page 44 in chapter 2. The difference is that anticipatory anxiety means we are unconsciously but continuously thinking about and preparing for what might go wrong. This chronic anticipation of big and small problems needing to be solved—before they arise—stems from our deeply ingrained compulsion to manage the things, people, and situations around us. Our minds are always active, constantly projecting into the future as a means of feeling safe in the present. We fall under the unconscious illusion that we can prevent whatever it is we don't want from happening if we fixate on it until we're fried. We may not even realize the stress we're carrying.

There are many reasons we may be prone to this type of anxiety, such as a parent or caregiver who modeled this behavior by chronically worrying about potential future issues or a chaotic childhood where anticipating what might go wrong was a way of staying safe. Anticipatory anxiety operates on such a low volume in daily life that we may not even realize it's there.

To create real change, we need to start noticing how and when anticipatory anxiety might be steering the ship. Incessant worrying about things that have not yet happened (and may never!) is obviously not helpful. It creates what I call "life lite." When half of our brain is caught up in the complex act of plotting and planning, we are not present. This makes life half as satisfying, juicy, and fulfilling. Just half of what it should be. Because we're only *half* there.

Being present requires us to feel all the feelings. And anticipating, planning, and doing spares us from sitting with our feelings because we're in action. This doesn't have to be our reality. As we acknowledge the role of low-level anxiety, we begin to see the full picture—and have the opportunity to stop *future tripping* and be more present to what is actually happening.

Say It with Me 💬

I release the need to constantly anticipate what might go wrong, allowing myself to live more fully in the present moment.

Secondary Emotions

Often what we perceive and experience as anxiety is in fact our response to more primary, raw emotions that we find difficult to articulate or process (such as fear, rage, grief, etc.). In other words, anxiety acts as a veil, a *secondary emotion* that obscures more difficult, primary feelings that threaten to overwhelm us. When we fear loss, being found inadequate, or being abandoned or rejected, we might unconsciously use anxiety to cover up these trickier internal experiences. Then, we can get confused about what we're *really* feeling. This leads us to misunderstand and misname (and often avoid) our true emotions.

When we can recognize when anxiety is the secondary emotion, we have the opportunity to peel back our protective layers and explore and acknowledge what is actually driving our behaviors. We venture deeper into our inner self, to confront and embrace the depth of our real feelings.

By doing so, we're not just transforming our experiences, we're also recalibrating our nervous system. And by not rejecting our own responses, we allow our bodies to shift from a state of constant alertness and stress to one of resilience and presence. We know that we will show up for whatever happens and however we feel about it. Herein lies our path to a more balanced life, one that is mentally, emotionally, and physically healthier—and ultimately more secure.

BACK TO YOU
Naming and Identifying Secondary Emotions

One of the most powerful tools in emotional regulation is simply identifying and naming the emotion you are feeling. Often we misidentify secondary emotions—those that are fueled by other, deeper feelings—as primary emotions.

Take anger, for instance. It often masks other, more vulnerable emotions such as hurt or sadness. Many people find it easier to express anger because it conveys a sense of strength, whereas acknowledging feelings of hurt or sadness can make us feel exposed or weak.

To enhance emotional understanding and resilience, it's crucial to delve deeper, asking, "What emotions are fueling my anger?" This introspective approach helps in accurately identifying and addressing the root emotions, leading to more authentic and constructive emotional expression.

List five different emotions you have felt recently. Be specific. Rather than using broad words like "bad" or "good" use more precise terms, like sad, hopeless, ashamed, or anxious.

Do you allow yourself to feel a full range of emotions, or do you stifle some? Be sure to expand on your answers.

Emotional Self-Regulation

Emotional self-regulation is the ability to have a certain amount of healthy self-control over our own emotional state. I don't mean the kind of control where we just shut feelings down, but where we recognize our feelings, relate to them in a healthy way, and respond accordingly.

Without emotional self-regulation, life can be unnecessarily stressful and feel out of control. Our emotions can overwhelm us, blocking our ability to respond thoughtfully. When I was a talent agent in New York, I was perpetually in a rush, even when I had plenty of time. I would arrive at my office frazzled and already filled with angst before the day even began. My behavior was driven by an illogical fear of being late and was so habitual I had no idea that I was *choosing* my distressing morning experience. In therapy, my frequent complaints about my nightmarish subway commute with rude, inefficient people ("step into the car already, buddy!"), inspired Bev to give me homework to strengthen my emotional self-regulation.

For an entire week, she told me to add thirty minutes to my commute time and to intentionally be the last person to board the train. This meant consciously letting go of my usual calculated positioning at the exact right spot where the doors opened and pushing past others to be one of the first on. At first, it seemed impossible to approach my commute this passively, because it somehow felt like I was losing something. But I was motivated to see if I could leave the daily stress sesh behind. I soon discovered that I could. It felt amazing to stop rushing everywhere all the time. The positive ripple effect impacted many other areas of my life where I was also on racing-to-the-finish-line autopilot. I could suddenly see that I had options. Even if I could barely resist the urge to indulge an ingrained behavior, Bev's homework taught me I always had a choice. And so do you.

A key element to successfully interrupting behavior patterns is to slow down. When our response is compulsive or reactive, there's no space to do anything differently. For example, if you never let a text message, email, or voicemail sit—and if not responding immediately creates pressure or anxiety in you—it's time to adopt a different way. We are on edge thinking we have to respond right away, and we also are training other people about what to expect from us—in this case, total availability. If we build in time and space to reflect, think, and expand, then we can decide how available we want to be and to whom.

Say It with Me 💬
I trust in my ability to navigate life's challenges
and emotions with grace and presence.

Navigating Emotional Activation

Before we get to full acceptance of our emotional depths, however, we first have to deal with where we are *now*. Often, we live in a state of extreme busyness, on high alert, swiftly moving onto the next thing. In this state, we don't have a chance to slow down and respond thoughtfully.

Emotional reactivity is very common. It means we don't have any space between when something happens and when we respond to it. Something happens, we react. There is no pause, no moment to consider how things are going to go. For example, your busybody colleague—who reminds you a lot of your mother—drops by your cubicle to let you know, in a self-important tone, that it's your turn to tidy the office kitchenette. Fixing her with a steely glare, you say, "Betty, I'm busy. Besides, it's not even my week." This is an automatic reaction. Whether it's true or not, you want Betty off your case *now*. (Meanwhile, Betty sends out an office-wide email about *some people*, and the situation escalates.) We *always* have a choice in how we respond. But when we're emotionally reactive, this doesn't seem like an option.

In your life as a high-functioning codependent, there will undoubtedly be times when containing your feelings seems impossible. Someone may say or do something that pushes your buttons, sending you from zero to sixty, emotionally. If you had a punitive parent, you might find yourself particularly upset by a friend's judgmental comments, more so than someone without this family background.

When we are emotionally reactive, caught in instant, highly charged reactions, we can attack, blame, name-call, analyze, pursue, or yell. We can also withdraw and isolate, deny and stonewall, or go numb because we do not know how to share, process, or manage our feelings. As a result, our feelings end up managing us, and we defend or avoid. For example, we might withdraw in anger after an argument and refuse to discuss what happened. This reactive behavior blocks real problem-solving and can create tension and unfinished business in relationships.

Over the years, Randi's team had persistently tried to take over the responsibility of handling the late-night crisis calls to the domestic violence hotline from her. Despite their capability and eagerness to help, her emotional reactivity would kick in and she would immediately react with a hard *no* accompanied by detailed justifications for why she felt it had to be her.

Not everything is a code-red emergency, even though it can feel that way when our emotions are dysregulated. Being in a perpetual state of emotional reactivity—a primal survival mode—is also draining and can ultimately lead to burnout.

I did an Instagram live with conscious parenting expert and *New York Times* bestselling author Dr. Shefali Tsabary, where she insightfully pointed out, "One hundred percent of the time when we are triggered by people, places, and things, it is because of us." This means the source of our trigger lies within us, shaped by our earlier experiences, perceptions, and inherent temperament. This realization is empowering and liberating. When we recognize that our reactions stem from internal sources, we gain more control over how we respond. We are no longer at the mercy of the world, getting our emotional circuits jammed up while reacting to everyone's insensitive comments and behavior. Sure, Betty might be behaving like a bossy know-it-all, but the reason she triggers you is really about *you*.

Having the skills to emotionally self-regulate amid intense reactions can help protect our own peace and happiness. That's why self-regulation is a cornerstone of emotional resilience. Recognizing this allows us to navigate life with a heightened sense of clarity and calm, transforming our experience from being at the mercy of our triggers to mastering our emotional landscape.

BACK TO YOU
Navigating Emotional Triggers

When something or someone triggers a heightened emotional response in you, step back and ask yourself the following 3Qs for Clarity. These questions will help you identify the original source of your triggers, and how your present response is rooted in past (unresolved) experiences:

1. Who does this person remind me of?

2. Where have I felt this way before?

3. Why is this behavioral dynamic familiar to me?

By understanding the past dynamics fueling your current triggers, you become less susceptible to them. Once you recognize that you're being activated or triggered, the next step is to decode your reaction. This keeps your emotional responses firmly on your side of the street, where you have a greater chance of communicating your feelings healthily and directly.

When we learn to self-regulate, we notice our feelings in the moment and have the staying power to sit with them. We can shift from reacting to observing, seeing ourselves as distinct from whatever emotion is coming up. Shifting language from "I'm so anxious" to "I'm having anxious feelings" can also help to separate us from an overwhelming feeling we might be having. Creating space like this is a form of emotional self-regulation. It helps us take things less personally. That doesn't mean that someone's passive-aggressive behavior won't get on our nerves (ugh, Betty!), but it does mean that we can pause, breathe, and not take it on. Simply watch it and decide how to respond.

Here's what emotional self-regulation can look like:

- **The ability to calm yourself** (taking a few deep breaths and practicing mindfulness techniques when you feel overwhelmed, reminding yourself that this too shall pass)

- **The ability to cheer yourself up when you feel down** (engaging in self-soothing activities like listening to uplifting music, practicing positive affirmations, or focusing on moments of joy from the past)

- **Communicating openly, effectively, and truthfully** (expressing your feelings and needs in a calm and assertive manner, rather than reacting impulsively or keeping your emotions bottled up)

- **Acting in accordance with your values** (for example, choosing to prioritize your health and well-being by sticking to an exercise routine even when you don't feel like it, because it aligns with your value of self-care)

- **Persisting through difficulty** (facing a challenging situation or setback with determination and resilience, knowing that setbacks are a part of growth and learning)

- **Putting forth your best effort** (giving your all in your personal and professional endeavors, even when faced with obstacles, because you value excellence and self-improvement)

By knowing ourselves emotionally and trusting ourselves enough to be honest about how we sincerely feel, we open the door to others accurately knowing us, too.

The Shadow Self

When it comes to developing a healthy relationship with our emotions, we have to examine where hidden shame might be playing a role. In chapter 3, we explored what shame is (feeling inherently bad or unworthy) and how its toxic influence affects our ability to heal old wounds and confidently operate in our lives. Shame can also be devastating to our healthy emotional expression, especially if we feel ashamed of our needs or feelings.

The experience of shame goes hand in hand with our shadow selves. The term *shadow self*, coined by Carl Jung, represents the parts of ourselves that we've repressed or denied—typically traits or emotions that we deem unacceptable or incompatible with our conscious identity. For example, it's uncomfortable to admit our tendency to lose our temper, to make unfair or unkind judgments, or to place blame on others instead of taking responsibility.

As your shadow becomes clearer, you may experience feelings of sadness, shame, anger, or frustration. Although the parts of yourself you have been denying might indeed feel threatening to acknowledge at first, they also liberate you from stuck patterns and being shut down.

Allow the feelings to be present and to move through you. Remember that you are not your feelings; they *will* pass. As uncomfortable as they might be, there is a power in real self-acceptance—which means truly seeing who we are in our niceness and not-so-niceness. We are all works in progress, flawed and beautiful simultaneously.

I had a client who felt highly activated by her partner's lack of professional initiative and his tendency to under-earn. Initially, her frustration seemed to be exclusively toward her partner's behavior, but deeper exploration revealed a shadow aspect. We discovered that she had repressed her anger about always having to be the responsible one (a childhood family role) and carried a hidden fear of not being cared for. Recognizing these aspects shifted the focus from blame and frustration to a perspective of understanding and self-compassion. This opened a calm dialogue between them about her feelings and steps he could take to make their shared fiscal life more equitable.

When we embrace and engage our shadow, we also diminish its power to control us unconsciously. It's like bringing light into a dark room—the fears and negative emotions lose their intensity and become manageable. This integration is crucial as it facilitates a more holistic and balanced approach to life.

BACK TO YOU
The Shadow Self

To begin to uncover your shadow self, take a minute or two to follow the steps below.

Step 1: Investigate. Answer the following questions:

- What qualities do you dislike the most in others?

- In your life, whom do you gossip about most often? Why?

- What frequently irritates you about your interactions with other people?

Step 2: Flip the script. Now ask yourself how the qualities you just identified show up in yourself. Spend a few minutes writing out what you discover. For example, if Betty is always mad at someone, and it irritates you, consider how you might often be angry at the people around you.

Identifying and accepting what we've been denying in ourselves helps us to become fully integrated and whole again. It liberates repressed energy and provides more fuel to fully live your unique life.

Defense Mechanisms

Just as we disavow our shadow selves, we use *defense mechanisms* to protect ourselves from feeling discomfort, guilt, or anxiety. These feelings can arise if we feel threatened or internally conflicted. The mind is unconsciously wired to shield us against anything that inspires discomfort or pain, so it finds ways to twist the reality of what *is*. While we can see the good intentions here (to protect), defense mechanisms can distance us from our true emotions and self.

It is important to note that, for the most part, we resort to defense mechanisms unconsciously. Still, if they go completely unexamined, they can block our ability to create healthy relationships with robust boundaries. The good news is that we can become aware of how our unconscious mind has been protecting us from stressful feelings and situations. That awareness can create the possibility for mindful choices.

Projection. As we covered in the "Shadow Self" section above, projection is when we assign a feeling or quality to another person that we deny within ourselves.

Have you ever heard the saying, *If you spot it, you got it*? That means we are projecting our shadow onto other people. If you are a parent and you find that one of your kids pushes your buttons exceptionally well, it could be that your kid is expressing qualities that you've suppressed.

Another way we project is by attributing feelings, motives, desires, and attitudes that we deem unacceptable onto others. You may say, "I don't think Betty likes me. She made a face when I said hello," when the reality is that it's *you* who doesn't like Betty (who may not have given that interaction a second thought, btw).

When we reject parts of ourselves and project our unconscious emotions onto others, we push our shame and other undesirable emotions down even further—unconsciously strengthening the barrier to feeling whatever it is we might really need to be feeling. We are unconsciously trying to spare ourselves pain, but the cost—a skewed understanding of what's going on in and around us—is substantial.

Other common defense mechanisms are:

- **Denial:** When our mind can't bear a feeling or situation that is too painful (and possibly requires action), we outright reject the reality of whatever we can't accept— our failing marriage, our friend's obvious mental health struggles, our child's addiction, etc. In denial, we're avoiding the emotional impact of what is actually happening.

- **Displacement:** We transfer our negative and overwhelming feelings onto someone or something else. An example: someone has a crappy day at work and takes it out on a customer service rep.

- **Rationalization:** When we employ rationalization, we're attempting to construct acceptable excuses for unacceptable behavior. We can apply rationalization to ourselves or others. An example of rationalization might be your partner exploding at you over something small and you justifying their outburst by saying they are under extreme stress at work—rather than acknowledging their inappropriate behavior.

- **Sublimation:** This is a defense mechanism that involves channeling unwanted feelings or unacceptable urges into an activity that is appropriate, safe, and oftentimes positive and productive. An example of sublimation might be a person with anger issues channeling that energy into competitive sports instead of lashing out at others verbally or physically.

Learning to go within and accept, allow, and acknowledge all of our emotions without judgment is key to liberating ourselves from emotional confusion so we can relate from a clear-eyed, honest place.

It took Randi, my superwoman client, some time to recognize that although she felt satisfaction from her work, she was overly identified with her clients and not in touch with her own feelings. In therapy, Randi faced a profound realization: her relentless drive was fueled not just by her admirable passion, but also by sublimation. This defense mechanism had her channeling the trauma of her childhood—years spent navigating the uncertainty of shelters—into her all-consuming advocacy work. It was a noble redirection of her emotions, yet it left her with no time to connect with her own feelings or desires.

Her work was also leading to an unrealistic and urgent schedule (including immediately responding to middle-of-the-night calls and emails) that left no time or space to focus on herself and her internal life.

As we continued our work together and delved into her past, Randi learned to articulate and process her emotions, a journey that was both painful and liberating. As she developed more ability to experience what she genuinely felt, she cried, she raged, but most importantly, she began to heal.

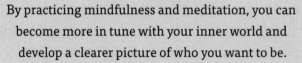

Loving Reminder 🖤
By practicing mindfulness and meditation, you can become more in tune with your inner world and develop a clearer picture of who you want to be.

Learning to Tune In

According to Jon Kabat-Zinn, the founder of Mindfulness-Based Stress Reduction (MBSR) training, "Mindfulness is awareness that arises through paying attention, on purpose, in the present moment, nonjudgmentally in the service of self-understanding and wisdom." Mindfulness practices like meditation, self-reflective journaling, body scans, breathing exercises, and nature walks are powerful tools to redirect our anxious leaning into the future. But that's not because these practices completely empty the mind of its future-oriented thoughts. Rather, we "see" and hear at last what our thoughts actually are. By acknowledging what's constantly racing through our brains—influencing our feelings, actions, and reactions—and consciously choosing to let them pass without engaging with them, we can sidestep their influence. We see that we have a choice.

Mindfulness is a process of learning to be truly present. That means allowing life to unfold more naturally with less need to steer it to avoid something or create something. Less management of people and outcomes creates more space to fully *be*. Our ability to regularly *be here now* will also transform our experience from a "lite," half-present version of life to its richest, most fulfilling expression.

As I did for many of my clients, I introduced Randi to the idea of doing a guided meditation at the end of our sessions. Many of my non-meditator clients were able to develop a dedicated practice and increase their internal calm by starting in my office. At first, Randi insisted that she was not a "meditator" and confessed that she had tried and failed to get a practice going multiple times. "I'm hopeless!" she said, shaking her head. "I know people love it but—I just cannot empty my mind of thoughts." Once we established that being devoid of thoughts was not the point, and that all she needed was the willingness to try, Randi relaxed.

My office was intentionally cozy, to encourage the kind of relaxation and trust that we all need to go inward. I had decorated it with twinkle lights, soft throw blankets, and lavender candles. Clients knew it as the Zen Den, a safe space where they could let go of the world and be themselves. Randi was no exception; she would audibly exhale as she entered the space and sink into the couch. She started looking forward to our meditation time during which I would interweave the important themes of the session and record the guidance for her to use at home. It took a few weeks until she was ready to incorporate meditation into her life outside of our sessions. She excitedly set up her own Zen Den at home, a sacred space just for her daily mindfulness practices.

BACK TO YOU
Create Your Zen Den

A Zen Den is an external sacred space that reminds you to tend to the divine sacred space within. Taking the time to create somewhere in your home (it can be a whole room or just one small side table) that soothes and nourishes you and has a positive ripple effect. Make it a comfortable, cozy, part of your self-loving experience.

Below are a few ideas of what you might put in your Zen Den. Feel free to add your own, too. After all, this is your special space. Have fun and enjoy what you create.

Fairy lights	Candles (be safe!)
Essential oils	A soft, fuzzy blanket or cushion
Your journal	Pictures of loved ones
Crystals	Plants

Flowers, leaves, or other natural seasonal items

My own path to establishing a daily meditation practice was long and winding. I loved the idea, but actually *doing* the thing (sitting down every day) turned out to be a stretch. While therapy with Bev definitely got me on the path to healing, I also wanted something outside of therapy that would be the mind-calming equivalent of my daily workouts at the gym. I got so into it that I created an inviting space, inspired by images I cut out from *Architectural Digest*, with gorgeous pillows, bottles of pure essential oil, an array of meditation music, and sage to clear any negative energy. I felt amazing in there. But I was also a bit like a sports enthusiast who buys all the clothes, shoes, and equipment, but barely gets on the court: I was all gear and no game. I had a beautiful space; the only thing I didn't have was an *actual* practice.

It wasn't until I met my teacher, Davidji, that meditation stuck. I met him along with Deepak Chopra at a Weekend Within program at the Chopra Center, a gift getaway from one of Vic's friends. Davidji described meditation as taking a thimble full of stillness and silence from our practice and infusing it into the rest of our day, which sounded amazing to me. He also invited the group to commit to twenty-one days of meditation when we returned home. If we didn't like it, we could quit. *I can do anything for twenty-one days*, I thought. And he was right: when I sat for thirty minutes early in the morning and early evening, it changed the other twenty-three hours of the day for the better. I slept better, had more tolerance, and became less reactive. I started being able to insert a pause before I responded to anything, even entitled behavior from coworkers or drama with my family. Responding mindfully instead of reacting instantly changed my relationships, my work—and my entire life. Meditation became one of the cornerstones of my therapy and coaching work. Davidji taught me to put all that gear to good use by teaching me to meditate in a way that finally worked for me.

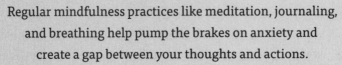

Loving Reminder 🖤
Regular mindfulness practices like meditation, journaling,
and breathing help pump the brakes on anxiety and
create a gap between your thoughts and actions.

Before therapy, Randi's work and time with her son were her main sources of joy. As she started to see more clearly and pay attention to her cues of unease and anxiety, she could self-soothe and felt confident enough to say what she desired out loud. Meditation became a gateway, allowing her to step away from the urgency of her work and into a tranquil space of self-discovery and reflection. Through this reflection, she realized she wanted her family to be a part of a community. She joined a neighborhood group of single parents and their kids and started to enjoy weekend outings, potluck dinners, and game nights with other families. She even surprised herself by agreeing to join a week-long group trip to Disneyland.

Like Randi, when you learn to welcome and accept your messy emotions, you enter a vibrant world of nuance, richness, and meaning. You learn to savor life's contrasts, where loss and sorrow can help you appreciate love and joy. By deeply knowing your emotions, you will naturally begin to engage in behaviors and responses more aligned with your desires, values, and the life you are creating.

Resistance and Self-Soothing

As you begin to shift toward healthier behaviors, expect to encounter emotional resistance during this time of transition. While you make gains, some part of you may not want to change the status quo. This natural aversion may manifest in subtle ways: exhaustion, avoidance, or self-sabotaging. It might show up as old habits coming back to life, or appointing yourself the "expert," advising others while neglecting your own advice, etc. It's a normal part of the journey.

Stay the course. This resistance, often operating unconsciously, can become more intense as we're nearing our goals. Acknowledging this, we can anticipate and prepare for all the ways resistance shows up, spot it, and move forward with our healthy choices in spite of it.

Learning to Self-Soothe

Our ability to make mindful, healthy choices increases exponentially when our nervous systems are relaxed. Have you ever found yourself tied up in knots over a decision and decided to table the issue until after you got a good night's sleep? Everything truly is better when our body and mind are at ease. More than that, having a plan to self-soothe regularly and intentionally before any emotional or life disruptions can make all the difference. That way, you can calmly manage your feelings and respond to situations instead of reacting. With more internal calm you are less likely to act out or numb out. Self-soothing doesn't have to be complicated or time-consuming. Even small, deliberate steps can significantly impact our ability to return to a state of equilibrium after emotional disturbances.

Here are some of my favorite ways to self-soothe:

- **Change the Environment:** When in distress, leaving the area, even briefly, for a walk or nature immersion helps reset the nervous system.

- **Warm Baths or Showers:** As a practice, warm baths, enhanced with bath salts and candles, offer a transformative sensory experience. Showers also effectively refresh and reset.

- **Mini Grounding:** This concise and powerful method is designed to anchor you amid stress. Begin by taking three deep, deliberate breaths, ensuring your feet are firmly connected to the earth beneath you. Proceed to dial into your five senses, one at a time, merely acknowledging what you are experiencing, sense by sense, without judgment (*I see . . . I hear . . .* etc.).

- **Breathing Exercises:** Deep breathing curbs cortisol release and stabilizes the heartbeat. I use the Pause Breathwork App for its simplicity, especially when overwhelmed.

- **Express Soothing Preferences:** Share and understand soothing preferences with loved ones. Like love languages, everyone has unique ways to find solace.

- **Humming:** Use humming or gargling to soothe anxiety and stimulate the vagus nerve (the main nerve cluster of the parasympathetic nervous system), promoting relaxation. It's free, easy, and available anytime.

- **Micro-moments:** Amid busyness, cherish micro-moments, like smelling jasmine oil or taking deep breaths to teach your nervous system to unwind.

> ### Say It with Me 💬
> I am more and more secure in my ability to
> handle whatever comes my way.

When resistance hits, remember that awareness is your ally in this journey. View setbacks as learning opportunities and part of a growth mindset that gradually reshapes our perspective and overrides our *negativity bias* (our natural human tendency to give more weight to negative information and experiences than neutral or positive ones). Embrace this learning process, and let your interactions, even the challenging ones, enrich and reshape your understanding.

Randi continued with her most important work—getting to know herself on deeper levels. For a long time, she had operated on passion- and purpose-driven autopilot, but step by step, she learned to bring her emotional reality to the forefront of her awareness. This helped her to tolerate her feelings and *act mindfully* instead of compulsively *reacting*. A huge indication of her growth was voluntarily delegating the overnight emergency calls to her highly capable staff. She finally got that *it did not always have to be her.* As she took better care of her emotional self, she had the energy and drive to continue building her social relationships along with a deep sense of belonging for both herself and her son. For the first time in her life, she knew herself and felt truly present. For the first time, she was living her life by her design.

▶ TAKE ACTION ◀

- **Top of Mind.** Pay attention to your emotional responses over the next few days. If you get activated and have an amplified response to an experience, stop to decipher the meaning by using the 3Qs for Clarity tool on page 148. Our triggers can be a meaningful opportunity to have a deeper understanding of ourselves and what drives us.

- **Take Care.** Take a moment to laugh. Watch funny videos, movies, or some stand-up comedy. Laughter is a great stress reliever.

- **Go Deeper: Take an Emotional Inventory.** Understanding our emotions is key to personal growth and healing. Go to page 245 in the "Go Deeper" section at the back of the book to gain insights into your emotional patterns to help you navigate your feelings more effectively.

CHAPTER 8

Establishing Good Boundaries

"I CAN'T SLEEP. That's why I'm here."

Cecilia was no-nonsense. Her voice carried the unmistakable accent of Bensonhurst, Brooklyn, the Italian neighborhood where she was born and raised, and still resided. Her heritage was palpable, not just in her tone but in her every gesture and in the passionate way she spoke about her family. Now, the same brownstone building that housed her life's stories was also the silent witness to her recent struggle with insomnia.

As we settled into the session, I assured Cecilia I could offer practical tools like guided meditations and evening wind-down routines to help her get back on track. But I also thought delving deeper into the root cause of her restlessness would be beneficial.

As her story unfolded, she spoke of waking up exhausted for the fifth morning in a row. She'd wanted to sleep late but was thwarted by a commitment to make pasta sauce early in the morning—a routine deeply rooted in her culture, where food is synonymous with care and love.

"Sauce?" I asked, confused as to why a retiree had to wake up early to cook. "Was it for some kind of event or volunteer project?"

"No, nothing like that," she said. "It's for my son. I make him sauce every week."

I paused for a moment. I needed to know more about her relationship with her adult son.

When Michael first moved to Manhattan, he was young and totally overwhelmed by his early career in finance, so every Saturday morning, he'd drive back to Bensonhurst where his mother would do his laundry and supply him with pasta sauce for the week. Doing those things was a way for Cecilia to support her son while staying in touch. Plus, she could rest easy knowing he always had something to eat and clean clothes to wear.

Years later, Michael was in his early thirties and established in his work. He could easily find other ways to cook and clean for himself. Yet she felt powerless to change their unspoken agreement. Her phrase "he's just so busy" became a mantra, an excuse that perpetuated the cycle, even as it intruded on her sense of autonomy. Her generosity had morphed into an obligation.

Cecilia needed to establish a boundary. But when I broached the subject, she hesitated, her eyes reflecting the conflict within. "I don't even know where to begin," she admitted. "Won't setting a boundary make me seem . . . selfish?" she asked. I assured her that sharing her truth with Michael was actually the opposite of selfish.

Knowing when and how to set boundaries can be perplexing, but it's crucial for both our own health and the health of our relationships. It can feel daunting at first, maybe even impossible. Most of us don't want to be labelled as demanding or difficult, self-absorbed or controlling, so instead of saying what we really want or mean, we present as go-along-to-get-along, saying things like, "It's all good! You know me, I'm easy." That easy-breezy mask might give us momentary peace, but in the long term we wind up feeling lonely, misunderstood, and resentful.

Boundaries are one of the cornerstones of our overall well-being. No matter how challenging it might feel to master them, you *can* do it. And, as you start to focus more on your own preferences, you will start to worry less about other people's perceptions of your choices.

Boundaries 101

Having boundaries means communicating clearly to the people in your life about what is okay and what isn't okay with you. It's telling the truth about how you feel and about what you want and need.

But if you were raised in a family system with disordered boundaries (and let's be honest, most of us were), it can be challenging to know where you need boundaries, and more difficult to effectively establish and enforce them. You can't expect yourself to have mastery over something you weren't taught. (My first book, *Boundary Boss*, is your one-stop shop for all things boundaries. Visit boundarybossbook.com for the deep dive.) What I've found in over two decades as a psychotherapist is that most of us received some seriously bad intel about boundaries.

Here's a simple way to think about them: a fence around a house is a boundary. It denotes the property line, shows what belongs to you (house, car, garden) and what does not (sidewalk, streetlights, road, etc.). Personal boundaries are like the fence around the "house" that is you. It shows other people where your personal space begins and ends, what behaviors you accept, and how you expect to be treated. The thing is, you have to establish your "fence" with your actions, body language, and actual words since it's not something visible.

Your boundaries are as unique as you are. Clearly communicating your boundary preferences, desires, limits, and deal-breakers is like sharing your own "rules of engagement" with others. They transparently identify permissible ways for others to interact with you and set relationships up to succeed.

There are five main types of boundaries:

- **Physical:** How you prefer to keep your personal space; how much privacy you require; and how you prefer others to interact with you physically (e.g., hug, handshake, or neither?).

- **Sexual:** How you prefer to be touched, practice consent, and experience intimacy.

- **Material:** How you relate to your possessions; whether you give or lend things, like clothes, money, computer, food, and even your toothbrush.

- **Mental:** How you share your thoughts, values, and opinions. Knowing what you believe and being able to stand firm in your beliefs, even when others disagree or disapprove. Being flexible enough to see another point of view as well.

- **Emotional:** How you take responsibility for your emotions and distinguish them from someone else's. Not feeling guilty or responsible for feelings that are not yours. Refraining from giving or receiving unsolicited advice or blaming others.

Boundary Styles

We've established the five areas where we need boundaries. Now, let's move on to the three basic boundary styles. Below we will explore how each one shapes our interactions and personal boundaries.

- **Porous:** Porous boundaries are too malleable or loose and lead to overinvestment in the problems and issues of others and potentially saying yes when you want to say no to keep the peace. Unsolicited advice–giving and spontaneous fixing are indications of porous boundaries.

- **Rigid:** Rigid boundaries are too firm and inflexible, preventing you from asking for help or expressing vulnerability. They can keep even your closest people from knowing you intimately.

- **Healthy:** Healthy boundaries are the sweet spot in the middle. When you have healthy boundaries you value your own opinion; you can communicate your preferences, limits, and deal breakers; you don't compromise your values for others; and you can accept when others set limits or say no.

Most of us, especially HFCs, vacillate between styles depending on the situation. It is not uncommon to have healthy or rigid boundaries in your career but tend toward porous boundaries in romantic relationships.

→ CHECK IN

Let's dig a little deeper.

- *What type of boundary do you have the most difficulty setting (physical, sexual, material, mental, or emotional)?*

- *When you read the descriptions for boundary styles, which one did you relate to the most (porous, rigid, healthy)?*

Navigating Emotional Boundaries

Disordered emotional boundaries are one of the top issues for HFCs. Yet knowing how to navigate our emotions as distinct from others' emotions is an integral part of healthy relationships. Recognizing and maintaining healthy emotional boundaries helps us interact in a way that respects both our well-being and that of those around us.

As we have established, many HFCs identify as empaths or highly sensitive people. As such, they tend to struggle with porous emotional boundaries, absorbing others' emotions as their own and blurring the distinction between their feelings and those of others. When this occurs, they go into management mode. *I don't want my partner to get upset, so I won't share my true feelings*, or, *I'll just handle things to avoid a situation where they might get frustrated*, and so on. Anytime you notice yourself thinking about what you don't want others to feel, that's a cue to back up—not your side of the street.

For many of us HFCs, it's not only that we don't want others to feel a certain way, but that we can't *let* them feel a certain way. This indicates we're taking on emotional responsibility for another person. We may feel deep down that others' happiness is our responsibility, but by now you know that this is just not true. This limiting belief impedes our own growth and ability to make healthy choices for ourselves.

Emotional dog whistles are other people's subtle, nonverbal cues that signal displeasure, sadness, or anger, and which prompt a reaction. As HFCs, we are great at tuning in to the emotional energy of those around us. Our friend may wrinkle their nose at something we say, and so we instantly backpedal to fix whatever prompted that reaction. Meanwhile, they haven't actually said a thing.

When we have good emotional boundaries, we're able to unhook from compulsively reacting to what someone *might* be feeling and, if appropriate, ask questions to bring unspoken emotions out into the open, such as, "You seemed upset when I made a comment about this weekend. What's going on?"

As I shared in chapter 2, I was a boundary disaster when it came to my sister Jenna and her awful backwoods domestic situation. I hadn't realized what was missing until I asked my therapist Bev what else I could possibly do to "fix" the situation. She calmly replied, "Set a boundary to protect yourself." *What?*

Prioritizing my own emotional health had never entered my HFC mind. In fact, it was a terrifying prospect because it felt like abandoning Jenna in her time of need, which went against everything

I believed about being a supportive sister. With Bev's guidance, though, I committed to doing it.

I mustered up the courage and called Jenna and said, "Hey, I love you and continuing to hear about this guy's horrible treatment of you is just too painful. So just know that I'm going to step back, but if and when you are ready to get out, I am still your person. You say the word, and I'm there."

I wish I could say that it felt one hundred percent amazing. It didn't. Jenna's calls became far less frequent. It wasn't always easy, but setting that boundary helped me regain some internal peace. I had more time and bandwidth to focus on my own domestic life with my new family. I realized that by setting that boundary I was controlling what I could control: myself.

The foundation for healthy boundaries is developing an unwavering ability to know, honor, and protect yourself, so naturally your relationships are going to be impacted by any new behaviors you bring.

Through therapy I realized that attempting to solve someone else's problem is like going to the gym to cure someone else's diabetes. You can't do the work on someone else's behalf and expect them to get the results. I actually owed it to Jenna to back off. I owed it to myself, too. To make this change, I had to trust Bev, Jenna, and myself—a lot.

When you have the courage to speak honestly, you are no longer self-abandoning, acquiescing, or waiting with bated breath for the other person's approval. You become the person you can count on, someone who is strong enough to stand up for yourself and ultimately your relationships, too.

Every time you choose not to self-abandon, every time you withstand the discomfort of maybe disappointing someone, every time you assert your right to set a boundary and prioritize your needs, it's a win.

BACK TO YOU
Blocks to Setting Boundaries

Understanding why it's hard to set emotional and other boundaries is the first step in overcoming the obstacles. Let's explore the top five reasons that often make setting these boundaries difficult.

1. **Fear of Rejection:** You might avoid setting boundaries for fear that others will reject you or think you're being unreasonable. You may worry that by saying no or asking for what you need, you will be perceived as difficult or selfish.

2. **Lack of Self-Awareness:** You might not have a clear sense of your own needs and values, or you might struggle to articulate them. Without this awareness, setting boundaries effectively can be challenging.

3. **Guilt or Obligation:** You may feel guilty or obligated to say yes to requests or demands from others, even when it's not in your best interest. You might feel responsible for meeting others' needs and struggle to prioritize your own.

4. **Fear of Conflict:** Setting boundaries can sometimes lead to conflict or uncomfortable conversations. You might avoid this discomfort by not setting boundaries or by allowing others to cross your boundaries.

5. **Lack of Confidence:** You may not feel confident in your ability to set and enforce boundaries. You might worry that you will not be taken seriously or that others will push back against your boundaries. Without confidence, it can be difficult for you to establish and maintain healthy boundaries.

The Twenty-Four-Hour Rule

It is extremely common to experience *boundary regret* when you start setting boundaries. You might feel fearful, guilty, or anxious. You might feel really compelled to take it back. My suggestion is to make a commitment to yourself to not take anything back for twenty-four hours.

If you wait twenty-four hours post–boundary setting, the likelihood of you still wanting to take it back is usually small. Allow yourself to have a rollercoaster of emotions within the first twenty-four hours and be sure to self-soothe and take impeccable care of yourself.

Commit to this new boundary-setting cycle, and I promise you, you will be creating a new emotional standard for yourself. You will be normalizing making simple requests, prioritizing your preferences, and negotiating for your needs. The more often you go through the process, the easier it will be and the less boundary regret you will have.

Being Assertive

Asserting your truth by setting boundaries and having honest conversations supports your personal power.

To be assertive means speaking your mind and telling the truth about your experiences, needs, and feelings, even when you know the other party may not agree or even understand where you're coming from. It means asking for what is ideal for you, and what you would prefer, and saying no when you have to (or want to) without lashing out or otherwise misdirecting upset feelings.

When it comes to asserting your boundaries, a small step might be telling a pal that you'd love to pick a brunch spot that is halfway between your houses, instead of working on her assumption that you'll always come to her (um, because you have for the entire decade of your friendship). Or not twisting yourself up into a pretzel and ditching your hour-long run because your sister suddenly wants help choosing a new wall color for her dining room. Wherever you're in the habit of auto-yes-ing, slowly gravitate toward pausing, checking in with yourself, and speaking truthfully.

Being assertive is not the same as being aggressive. Nor does it mean being disrespectful. As HFCs, we may shy away from confrontation, but being assertive does not have to result in conflict. Quite the contrary. We can speak truth with ease, grace, love, and self-assurance, using simple, clear, and concise language. For example, if you were getting a massage and the therapist was using too much pressure, you might say, "The pressure is a bit too much for me right now. Could you please use a lighter touch?" Most massage therapists will be grateful for the honest feedback. You're also setting yourself up to fully enjoy the service you're paying for.

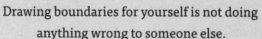

Loving Reminder 🖤
Drawing boundaries for yourself is not doing
anything wrong to someone else.

When Do You Need to Set a Boundary?

One of the most frequently asked questions I get from clients and students is, "How do I know when I need to set a boundary"?

If this is unfamiliar territory, you'll need to slow down and tune in. You might already have a feeling that something's not right, but not know what it is. The first step is to check your resentment. Feeling resentment is often a signal that you need to set or reinforce a boundary. For example, you may reluctantly say yes when a colleague asks you to stay late to help them meet their project deadline and then become resentful when you wake up exhausted the next day.

While outwardly, Cecilia continued her acts of service to support Michael willingly, inside, she held a secret belief that she was being taken advantage of and that her generosity was no longer appreciated. I encouraged her to conduct a "resentment inventory." Taking an inventory of where you might be harboring resentment in your relationships and why can provide a snapshot of where a need is not being met, where a boundary needs to be established, or where a boundary has been violated.

Next, it's important to tune in to your body wisdom. As HFCs, we tend to live in our heads, constantly thinking, but our bodies often know more about our boundaries than our minds do. We react immediately in a physical way when a boundary has been crossed or violated. For example, we might experience a constriction in the chest or a sick feeling in the stomach, a headache, or something else. For Cecilia, she ruminated and her mind raced when she tried to sleep.

Many of us are disconnected from our physical selves, making it challenging to tap into our body's wisdom. Cecilia's disconnection from her body resulted in her not canceling commitments (to Michael and others) when she was exhausted. She just kept going. With practice we can gain a deeper self-awareness and a more grounded presence in our own bodies (see chapter 9 for ideas). Then, finally, when we tune in to the unmet need that lies beneath the boundary violation, we can gain the clarity we need to set the right boundary.

BACK TO YOU
Take a Resentment Inventory

When we can connect the dots of what's bothering us to a specific incident, it will often reveal where a boundary has been crossed or a need has gone unmet. To take a resentment inventory, ask yourself the following questions.

☐ Is there anything I'm feeling resentful about right now?

□ What feels frustrating to me?

□ With whom do I feel upset, hurt, unheard, or unseen?

Use your answers to decide where you need to set or enforce boundaries.

As Cecilia and I continued our sessions, it became evident that her insomnia was not only related to the early mornings spent in the kitchen, but also to the silent contract she had with her grown son. Tapping into her resentment, she realized how much she felt unseen and undervalued. She wanted a less transactional, more voluntary relationship with her son. She was also ready to reclaim her time, her autonomy, and her peace of mind.

Over time, we discovered that Cecilia's need to help was somewhat of a compulsion, meaning that she couldn't resist helping. She volunteered at her church rectory three mornings a week, food shopped for her elderly neighbor, and volunteered at the local food bank. Discovering this was a lightbulb moment for her—what she thought she was doing purely out of love was actually driven by fear at times. She worried about would happen if she didn't do the things she saw as needing to be done for her neighbor and others. She did not want to find out, so she compulsively did them, including her weekly chores for Michael.

While it would be a bold new action to take, Cecilia agreed that setting a boundary was the next thing to do. The key, I explained, was not about finding the perfect words to say to Michael, or executing it flawlessly. It was about honoring her feelings, communicating clearly, and understanding that it was okay to be imperfect in the process.

We also started to imagine what might happen if she stopped doing chores for her son. What would be the best-case and worst-case scenarios? What would setting limits mean to her, and what would it mean to him? Could it change their relationship for the better?

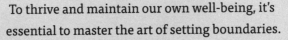

Loving Reminder
To thrive and maintain our own well-being, it's essential to master the art of setting boundaries.

Since knowing where and how to start can feel challenging, I introduced Cecilia to my four-step boundary plan.

Four Steps for Boundary Setting

Step 1. Get Clear Where a Boundary Is Needed. Cecilia would start by identifying where she felt resentment, using it as a compass to pinpoint where boundaries were needed.

Step 2. Pre-plan. Cecilia would consider the right time, place, and vibe to address her needs, taking into account her shared history with her son, in hopes that the conversation would be received in a spirit of understanding and respect.

Step 3. Craft a Boundary Script. Cecilia would prepare a clear and direct script to express her needs and desires without blame, using "I" statements to communicate her perspective.

Step 4. Visualize and Execute. Embracing the power of visualization, Cecilia would mentally rehearse the conversation and feel the empowerment of being heard and seen before having the dialogue with Michael. (Note: Regardless of how your boundary request is received, your healing is in asserting your authentic truth.)

When you communicate your boundaries clearly, you're actually setting the people in your life up to succeed. Boundaries become bridges, not blocks to deeper intimacy. They are about giving people the opportunity to know and love the real you. How can anyone love you authentically if you never allow them to know who you really are?

Say It with Me 💬
It's not my job to educate others on healthy boundaries.
It is my job to know and protect my own.

Armed with her newfound awareness and the four-step boundary plan, Cecilia felt prepared yet apprehensive about setting a new course in her relationship with Michael. It was a significant shift from her usual pattern of compulsively meeting others' needs to asserting her own.

This process was not just about changing her behavior, but also about reshaping the dynamics of their relationship.

With a deep breath and her carefully prepared script, Cecilia initiated the crucial conversation with Michael, stepping into a new realm of self-respect and mutual understanding. "Michael, you know I love cooking for you, but I need to start taking some time for myself. To do that, I won't be able to make sauce every week anymore. How about we make some together once a month?"

"I'm all for it, Mom," Michael replied. "I kept bringing my laundry and sauce jars because I thought you enjoyed doing them and I didn't want to hurt your feelings by stopping."

It may seem impossible that anyone could be so unaware that they believe, in their thirties, that their parent *wants* to do their laundry. But all of us at times are very unaware of what we're doing and what we're assuming. It doesn't mean that we are intentionally inconsiderate or oblivious. Folks like me and my sisters, who were once lazy teenagers avoiding dish duty, or Michael with his mom, were simply following the cues from the adults in our lives. Without guidance, clear boundaries, and expectations set by others, how can we possibly know what was needed or expected?

> ### Loving Reminder
> When we accept and respect others as autonomous individuals, we become less offended by their boundaries.

We Are Sovereign

Part of this journey is recognizing that even the people closest to us have the right to disagree or not want the things we want. They have the right to go through their own experiences, even if we may not appreciate how they're navigating them. My husband, Vic, and I handle our emotions very differently. If we have an upsetting disagreement, I need to talk. He needs time alone to think. After twenty-five years of marriage, I know he will come around to talking about it with me after a few hours. I tolerate my discomfort for a short time so I can respect his right to manage his emotions his way.

Learning to not make the other person's behavior all about me took years in therapy. If my college boyfriend so much as complained about a meal we had at a restaurant, I would feel defensive or even get angry at him. I would somehow feel responsible for his experience, even though that made no logical sense. After all, am I the one who cooked the food or owned the diner? Intellectually, it doesn't add up, and yet it's a common occurrence.

If someone sets a boundary that you don't understand, you can ask for clarity. You might ask for context by saying, "I want to understand better why you're not interested in joining us for dinner. Would you be willing to share more insight?" Again, you're not asking them to justify their decision, but if it's someone close and they say no to something important to you, it's okay to seek context or ask why. When you deliver these questions with a loving tone, without being demanding, people generally respond accordingly. It's all right to have questions.

Say It with Me 💬
Healthy emotional boundaries allow me to have compassion without taking on the feelings of others.

Respecting the Boundaries of Others

As HFCs-in-recovery, a key revelation is that being caring and kind toward other people does *not* require us to fix their problems. If we're used to being on autopilot, reacting instantly to everything and everyone in our environment, it can be challenging to perceive and respect other people's boundaries. Realizing that not only are our boundaries unclear, but that we *ourselves* can be terrible boundary crossers can come as a shock!

Imagine you walk by a mom at the grocery store. She's got a baby in one arm and a toddler walking by the cart. You see a few items fall to the ground, so you ask whether you can help her.

"I got it, thanks," she says. But instead of walking away, you watch her continue to struggle.

She asks her toddler to pick up the items, but he refuses.

So, again you ask, "Are you sure I can't help?"

Again, she reassures you that she's fine. Instead of accepting her answer, you walk over and say, "It's no problem, really," and pick up the items and drop them back into her cart.

Where is the boundary violation? It was kind to ask if the mom could use a hand. But it was a boundary violation to not accept when she declined the offer the first time. It was compulsive to fix a problem that she didn't want you to fix. You prioritized what you thought should happen by placing the items in her cart, over her expressed wishes.

Just as we have the right to refuse a request, we also have the responsibility to respect the limits or requests of others when the tables are turned, even when someone's refusal seems counterintuitive.

Maybe the woman wanted to take the time to wait for her toddler to place the items in the cart all by himself. Or maybe she simply did not want help. Either way, her reasons are her own.

BACK TO YOU
Are You a Boundary Bully?

Use the questions below to gently explore how often you might be inadvertently stepping over the boundaries of others.

☐ Do you respect the boundary requests that your partner, friends, family, or colleagues share with you?

☐ Have you unintentionally crossed someone's boundaries? What was the situation and what happened?

☐ How do you normally respond when someone tells you you've crossed a boundary? Do you get defensive, or do you listen and change your behavior accordingly?

☐ Have you ever asked your friends or family for honest feedback about how well you respect boundaries?

☐ What are three steps you can take to become more sensitive to other people's boundaries?

> Choose two to three of the questions above and journal about them to create a deeper understanding of how you're relating to the boundary requests of others.

Setting and respecting a boundary with someone we love dearly can feel especially challenging, yet the potential rewards are great. Nine months after I took my hands off the wheel of my sister Jenna's life—by letting her know that I was willing to help but needed to focus on my family in the meantime—the phone rang.

Jenna said, "I'm ready."

"Thank, God!" I said. "I'm getting in my car right now."

After leaving her a-hole boyfriend and his shack in the woods, Jenna stayed at a little lake cottage that Vic and I had winterized. She got into therapy, started attending AA meetings, and enrolled in school to become a certified nursing assistant.

When I finally declined to play the hero role in Jenna's story, she stepped up to become her own hero. That can be one of the biggest tragedies of being an HFC: when we insert ourselves as the hero of someone else's story, we potentially rob them of the wonderful things they are meant to accomplish or experience on their own.

Many years later, our relationship is free from the murky dynamics of unhealthy, unspoken boundaries. Would she have taken those steps in that relatively short time frame had I not stepped back? It's hard to say, but either way, this experience helped me get and stay clear about my responsibilities, surrendering to reality, and transforming my codependence into genuine caring for others, myself definitely included.

Confidence and Self-Validation

One of the biggest benefits of having healthy boundaries is developing the ability to speak up and communicate honestly. Doing this regularly builds real confidence, which is radiant and attractive. We all love to be around genuinely self-assured people. They are self-contained and self-possessed. As HFCs, developing and strengthening our authentic confidence is important. It takes confidence to step outside of habitual behaviors, and to tap into our true potential and begin creating a life and relationships that feel more aligned with our real selves.

This is where the power of self-validation comes in. Many of us can be chameleon-like in seeking approval from others. If you've ever said a version of, "I'm thinking about going to that conference, too!" when you actually dislike conferences, or, "Yeah, I was thinking about Cabo this year myself," when in fact you'd planned a staycation, you know what I mean. So, in creating a life tailor-made to your own specs, you'll need to move away from looking to others for validation and instead find more from within.

When we can validate our own feelings, experiences, needs, and desires, whatever Betty thinks of our life choices and general way of being matters a whole lot less. If you were raised in a dysfunctional family system, you may have learned that doing things for others meant receiving approval and love. While this may have served you then, it's not serving you now. If we learn to care a lot less about getting this external validation, it also means we expend far less mental energy on others, energy that we can pour into ourselves and our own constructive pursuits instead.

→ CHECK IN

Reflect on how you received approval and validation from your early caregivers. What did that teach you about how to get love?

When I first stopped drinking decades ago, being around drunk people was triggering. People with lowered inhibitions would start confessing things that they most likely wouldn't remember the next day and I sadly couldn't forget. I discovered that I couldn't be in that situation and keep my well-being intact. That meant I'd leave any gathering at the first sign of slurred words. At first, I worried that my friends and family would judge me or think I was being "holier than thou." In fact, I was just trying to stay right within. I discovered I could take care of my needs, regardless of how they chose to spend their Saturday night and what they might think of my choice (spoiler alert: my VIPs were and are super supportive). To this day, if I start to see anyone crossing the line from buzzed to trashed, I'm out. That's my rule, and if I hadn't learned to validate and honor my own need, I imagine I would have wasted a ton of emotional and mental energy over the years.

The more you validate yourself and your needs, the more your self-esteem grows, too. Self-esteem is that feeling that you can handle your life. That whatever life throws at you, you know deep down that you will be okay because you are capable of seeing yourself through. With good self-esteem, there's a sense of durability inside you that comes from feeling good about who you are on a core level. Your self-image is positive. This healthy core will protect you from harmful barbs, whether coming from another person, life, or your own inner critic. Robust self-esteem will also translate to genuine confidence.

In the weeks that followed our boundary-setting session, Cecilia experienced a profound transformation. Her insomnia, which had once felt like an insurmountable obstacle, began to fade. She was no longer waking up to the compulsion of duty, but to a newfound sense of freedom. This change had a ripple effect; her sleep improved significantly, and she relished choosing activities that she genuinely enjoyed, rather than those she felt obligated to perform. Cecilia and Michael decided to continue their sauce-making tradition, but only once a month, turning it into a special family occasion rather than a weekly chore. Additionally, they agreed to meet for breakfast once a week, dedicating this time solely to socializing and enjoying each other's company, with no domestic tasks involved.

It might feel intimidating to take your newfound confidence and boundary-setting skills and put them into action, but you can do this. So far, you have successfully survived every challenging situation and experience. Allow yourself to recognize your own strength. Tap into your inner courage. You're not alone on this journey. As you continue to master these skills, you're unlocking a world of liberation, passion, and joy. A life with less suffering and more happiness awaits. Slowly but surely, you'll get there, and I'll be here cheering you on every step of the way.

▶ TAKE ACTION ◀

- **Top of Mind.** Over the next forty-eight hours, focus on resisting the urge to respond immediately to anything (except emergencies, of course). This includes phone calls, text messages, DMs, etc. Notice how it feels to not react right away and what emotions or thoughts come up. This practice helps you become aware of your response patterns and the pressure to always be available, encouraging you to prioritize your own needs.

- **Take Care.** Have a mini dance party to your favorite upbeat song. Let loose, feel the rhythm, and let go of any stress or tension through movement.

- **Go Deeper: Practice Boundary Scripts.** Learning to set effective boundaries is the key to a balanced life, where your needs and well-being take priority. Go to page 246 in the "Go Deeper" section at the back of the book to engage in an exercise that will empower you to identify and implement boundaries that create space for what truly matters in your life.

CHAPTER 9

Real Self-Care

SELF-CARE WAS *the theme* (and struggle) of my life in 2020. For starters, I was writing *my very first* book, which, while very exciting, was also a whole new endeavor, with its own learning curve and challenges. Then, came *my very first* global pandemic. Talk about new territory! Making matters much worse, a week before the world went on lockdown, my self-sufficient and all-around awesome mom received a frightening cancer diagnosis. Any one of these things had the power to turn my well-established self-care routines upside down, but together they made a perfect storm.

As I'm sure you remember, those early COVID-everything-everywhere days were fraught, intense, and intensely activating. Not only was I feeling the heat to complete my manuscript on time, but as an empath/HSP/HFC-in-recovery, I was, like many of you, deeply affected by the suffering coming through on my phone screen and in news reports. Having to confront my mother's mortality on top of this chaotic global landscape felt unbearable.

While her oncologist felt she needed treatment immediately, traveling to a hospital for treatment put her at added risk of contracting COVID-19. She decided to delay treatment for a month until the situation got under control. It was the right choice, yet it was also hard because we knew that while she waited, her tumor was growing. She seemed content with this decision. Meanwhile my own anxiety cranked up several notches.

Even though I was breathing, eating, and sleeping self-care and boundaries (the subject of the book I was writing), my anxiety was so great that everything I knew—and taught—went out the window to focus on my mother's health.

This is not uncommon in times of crisis, especially a crisis that involves caregiving, the HFC's specialty. Our hard-won therapeutic gains and personal freedom recede into the background, and we default to our tried-and-true (if tiresome) behavioral patterns. In my case, my mother's health crisis had my fullest attention. The complete attention part was, in some ways, appropriate, and of course understandable. I love my mom and was determined to help her get the best care possible. What was not appropriate was how I went into full HFC *must-do-everything* overdrive.

Seeming to forget that I had three capable and loving older sisters, I wrangled control of the situation, especially once my mother was able to begin treatment. And I did this in spite of the fact that prior to my mother's diagnosis, I had little time to spare given my intensive book-writing schedule. What little time I had was earmarked for self-care: hikes with Vic and my sister, classes with my fave trampoline instructor, and the occasional ice cream break, in addition to my daily meditation practice. But this kind of life curveball torpedoed my self-care practices (and my commitment to walking my talk).

Under the intense pressure of my conflicting needs and obligations—writing the book, running my company, not getting COVID, and showing up for my mother in her time of need—I slid into an old mindset, led by a faulty guiding belief: *it has to be me.* That meant creating and orchestrating a "Janny is Healing" schedule of care between my sisters and nieces, so that my mother would always be surrounded with love. That might sound like there was some delegation involved, but trust me, there wasn't. I was on that calendar like it was my lifeline. Folks would sign up and then I'd reach out, check in, and want to be involved with every little detail, making suggestions for food, TV shows, or activities. Even though my sister, Jenna, took a temporary leave from her job as a certified nursing assistant to live with our mother during her treatment, I still did the two-and-a-half-hour round trip to take her for radiation treatments almost daily. On top of that, I reached out to pals who had healthcare connections or who had experience with her type of cancer. When I couldn't sleep, I scoured websites for available clinical trials, joined Facebook groups for caregivers who had loved ones with my mother's cancer, and WebMD'd myself into oblivion.

One day, when I was on the long drive to my mom's house, droning on about who needed to do what, my sister, Katie, finally said, "Hey, Ter, Mom is good. Jenna is *living with her*, and Jenna is more capable than either one of us when it comes to caregiving. It's her *profession*."

Of course, Jenna was more capable—she took care of the elderly for a living. My stress had nothing to do with Jenna's abilities. It had everything to do with backsliding into trying to manage my *own* feelings of fear and anxiety by actively attempting to control everything and everyone else. This was my old faithful strategy to feel safe in a situation that brought up so much helplessness. In the process, I'd tossed aside the practices that normally kept me centered and sane.

For most HFCs, real self-care, whether in a crisis or not, doesn't happen naturally. Becoming proactive, listening to our bodies, and prioritizing our feelings and needs is something we learn deliberately. Building regular self-care practices means having compassion for ourselves, cultivating true self-love, and regularly *considering ourselves*, our needs, and our desires, in any situation.

Self-Consideration + Care

Like me, you may revert to over-functioning and over-giving in stressful situations to feel safe and in control. Some part of us may know we're defaulting to unhealthy habits, tossing out exercise and downtime in favor of managing, inserting ourselves, and other HFC behaviors that don't serve us. We may eventually find ourselves out of balance—short-tempered, sarcastic, judgmental, and frazzled. Not exactly how we want to show up in our relationships.

To shift into healthier behaviors, it's critical to learn to prioritize self-care. That is the proactive part. Not waiting until we are depleted, angry, or sick. When I say "self-care," I don't necessarily mean getting a mani-pedi or indulging in a spa day. While those are nice things to do for ourselves, what I mean here includes the broader sense of self-consideration: giving ourselves ample space and regular support as a way of life.

Self-care means being able to say no when your body is telling you that you need rest. (Challenging if you tend to over-work or suffer from FOMO.) Self-care is giving yourself permission to feel what you feel, want what you want, and decide what you decide. It's your job to prioritize your own self-care and well-being. Contrary to how you might have been conditioned, self-care is not selfish. It's imperative.

Prioritizing self-care can feel daunting at first, maybe even impossible. But it matters because it is part of the foundation of our health and overall well-being. So, no matter how challenging it is to fit it into your life, with intention and effort (and putting things in your calendar) you can strengthen your self-care muscles and reap the rewards that come with it. For example, I invited a workaholic client suffering from back pain due to long hours at the computer to start a simple routine: fifteen minutes of daily movement. To her surprise, this small change not only alleviated her back pain, but she also lost twelve pounds within two months. More than that, she experienced a newfound mental clarity and developed a much healthier relationship with her work.

This perspective shift toward more honest self-consideration might inspire you to be more open in your relationships, too.

Because you are being more honest with yourself, you might be better able to tell your people what lights you up, what brings you joy, what you absolutely, positively love. Even preferences that seem small matter (like how you like to wake up early, or love eighties pop music, for example), because they're part of what makes you *you*. Not only do you have a right to share your unique, amazing self, but this is also your responsibility. You know by now that hoping others will guess what you need is setting yourself up for disappointment and your loved ones for frustration. Regular self-care opens up a whole landscape of possibilities for you to share yourself more authentically. As a living, breathing human you are entitled to take up space. We truly need the unique gifts you have to offer the world.

> ### Loving Reminder 🖤
> Being proactive with your self-care can protect you
> from resentment, burnout, and chronic illness.

Self-Love

The foundation for self-care is legit self-love. It really is the antidote to being actively HFC. There is a lot of talk out there on social media about just learning to "love ourselves more," as if then we will somehow have life magically figured out. But self-love is less of a *feeling* and more a way of life. It's not magical, it's actionable. Your level of self-love is evidenced in the tone of your internal self-talk, how you regard yourself, how you interact with others, how you relate to your accomplishments and skills, and how you handle compliments, among other behaviors.

Flip the Script. How do you talk to yourself when you make a mistake or when something goes wrong? Are you calm and supportive? Punitive and blaming? Take a moment right now to think about the tone and content of your inner dialogue in these situations. For many of us, the inner mean voice is so habitual we are not even aware that it is consistently commenting in the background of our thoughts. Many times, that voice is the internalized voice of childhood caregivers, teachers, or coaches. If your inner voice is harsh, it is draining your energy and doing damage to your self-esteem.

BACK TO YOU
Listen to Your Inner Dialogue

For twenty-four hours, notice how you talk to yourself. Any time you have a negative self-conversation, put yourself down, or call yourself a derogatory name, write it down.

Take a rubber band or hair tie and put it around your wrist. Snap it whenever you notice negative self-talk.

Then, pause and replace it with something loving, such as:

I am good enough.

I am valuable as is.

I was born worthy.

Or, come up with an affirmation that feels right for you.

Catching negative self-talk and replacing it right away is important. Even running in the background, it is powerful and will wear away at your self-worth.

Own Your Skills. Many of us were taught to be humble at all costs. Don't have a "big head" or get "too big for your britches." The underlying message is, *don't feel too good about yourself or others won't like you; don't threaten others with your brains and skills, and for God's* *sake, never brag!* These ingrained and limiting beliefs can cause us to disavow our hard work and unique talents. I used to always say how "lucky" I was in my entertainment career until my therapist called me out. She said, "So, you credit your success as an agent to luck? Didn't you work hard to get where you are?"

Immediately I said, "Yes, I did, and I did it on my own!" Bev helped me see that chalking up my success to "luck" was my way of not threatening anyone else. But it also meant not taking responsibility for (or feeling proud of) the career that I'd built on my own. Feeling proud of your hard work is healthy. Feeling good about yourself is healthy. Sharing your accomplishments with others is healthy. Allow yourself to own your accomplishments. It's honest. They are yours, after all.

Embrace Praise. Accepting praise or a compliment can be uncomfortable. You may have grown up in a family where you only heard when you were doing things "wrong," and praise was scarce. Or, you saw the adults in your life reject praise and compliments, or heard them say that praise was only for God. How often do you reject, diminish, make light of, or squirm your way out of a compliment? If this is resonating, here's a reframe: the next time someone gives you a compliment, remember, it is about *them* and *their* experience of you. Your boss has a right to say, "good job," without you pointing out how that job could have been done better, or saying it was a "team effort." No need to duck out of the praise. There is a powerful shift that happens when you can embrace and appreciate *being appreciated*. A simple, *thank you for noticing*, will suffice. The better you get at accepting praise the more this acknowledgement raises your self-worth and self-esteem.

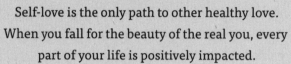

Loving Reminder
Self-love is the only path to other healthy love.
When you fall for the beauty of the real you, every
part of your life is positively impacted.

BACK TO YOU
Take a Self-Care Inventory

Let's do a quick investigation of your basic needs. Are they getting enough attention?

Consider what you might change in the areas of sleep, physical wellness, nutrition, hydration, downtime, meditation, journaling, etc.

- ☐ How much physical activity are you getting weekly? How does this align with your health goals?

- ☐ What specific situations or people inspire you to consider and take care of yourself? For example, if having dinner at a friend's place reminds you that you like to cook, how might you do more of that?

- ☐ How often do you check in with your emotions? What strategies do you use to process them?

- ☐ Identify any specific people or experiences that spark your own bad habits. For example, if going out for a drink never stops at one glass, what might need to change?

- ☐ Are you satisfied with your current eating habits? What changes, if any, do you think are necessary for better nourishment and nutrition?

- How much time do you dedicate to relaxation and leisure activities? How effective are these in reducing your stress?

- How often do you practice mindfulness or meditation? What impact does this have on your mental well-being?

- How would you rate the quality of your sleep? What steps could you take to improve it?

- How do you currently balance your work and personal life? What changes, if any, do you feel are necessary for better balance?

Ways to Boost Your Self-Consideration

Real self-consideration includes traditional self-care actions *and* psychological protection. Being discerning about our own energy, and what information and influences we allow into our consciousness, is powerful. The list of potentially damaging experiences is long and includes, but is not limited to, toxic relationships, the twenty-four-hour bad news cycle, spending our days on *get-it-done* autopilot, ignoring messages from our bodies, social isolation, being glued to our phone or other devices, and a steady flow of self-criticism.

Below is a menu of self-consideration habits to help you protect and nourish your energy levels and psychological well-being, which will improve the quality of your lived experience. Read through the list with an eye toward what you might do more of.

- **Insert a Pause.** While becoming more self-considerate, you will likely experience discomfort. Changing behavior takes patience because missteps, awkwardness, and failure are normal. It requires trusting that your effort is worth it. To weather this phase of things, it's helpful to learn to pause. Instead of drafting a sharp-tongued text, or exploding at a colleague over your morning coffee, learn to take a beat. Breathe. There's rarely any emergency out there; the urgency you feel is within you. You can handle the discomfort. And, those feelings will pass. Ask yourself, *What do I need to get back to my center?* If the answer is, *I don't know,* that's a valid answer. You don't have to act immediately. Taking simple, deep breaths can work wonders for getting balanced. The "win" here is not how events unfold out there, but that you've created some mental and energetic space. It's in this spaciousness that you can remember, *I have choices.* That's self-consideration in action.

- **Limit Doom-Scrolling and Other Distracting Content.** For the last few years, our world has been overwhelmed with, well, *overwhelm.* Thanks to our hyper-connectivity, we have unlimited access to more bad news, social media alarm bells, celebrity gossip, and general fearmongering than ever. But news sources and social media channels are places you can set limits to protect your mental health and general well-being. Maybe you allot fifteen minutes a day to catch up on what's going on in the world and then leave doom-and-gloom behind. Or, you might read the news in print form, or better yet, after your fifteen minutes turn off your phone and pick up a book. Learning to limit your intake of bad news and becoming aware of how you feel when you're, say, lost in the muck of things you cannot control or even influence are helpful ways to protect your energy and stay in your own lane.

- **Cultivate Body Wisdom.** Become habituated to tuning in to your visceral sensations. Learn to pay attention to the signals your body is giving you, for example, when your stomach is knotting up, or you feel a tightness in your chest or throat. If you're tired, give yourself the gift of rest, or of saying no, so you can say yes to your sanity and well-being. Sleep is an especially important part of being healthy in mind, body, and spirit.

- **Get Moving.** Our bodies need movement to function optimally. Try setting a timer on your phone to get up and stretch every hour or couple of hours. Put walking, fresh air, and stretch time on the daily menu of options. Your mind *and* body will thank you.

- **Meditate.** As you know by now, I'm a big fan of daily meditation. Even five minutes in the morning can make a *huge* difference in how you relate to yourself internally. Starting the day calmer and more centered has a positive ripple effect. If even five minutes seems impossible, you can do a walking meditation, being conscious of your breath and present to your surroundings as you move (without looking at your phone!). Any activity that brings you into deep focus for a period of time—such as cooking, needlepoint, running, even cleaning and sorting—is good training for meditation itself. Meditation is the greatest catalyst for making conscious choices, instead of compulsive ones.

- **Be Discerning about the Company You Keep.** We've all heard the old adage "misery loves company." Self-consideration in the social arena might mean being choosier about who you share your time and energy with.

If you have a close relative who is a chronic complainer, maybe don't call them in your ten-minute window of free time on a busy day. Yes, you still love them, but you're learning to love yourself, too.

- **Be Kind.** Nothing lifts the spirits like demonstrating interest, care, or compassion for another person. Genuine care does not require fixing anyone. You can add value to someone else's life and receive feel-good endorphins by doing something as simple as sending a pal who's struggling a soothing photo from your hike.

- **Stay Present and Have Compassion.** As we explored in chapter 7, relating to your emotions with compassion instead of judgment increases your ability to be a self-connected, self-caring human. When we are not mindful and loving toward ourselves, we tend to reach for quick fixes (as we mentioned in chapter 6) like a margarita, Netflix, social media, shopping, and, yes, being overly involved in the decisions of others. If a feeling becomes too overwhelming, ask yourself, *What is the message of this emotion? What is going on within that is making me feel this way?* Your openness and curiosity about why you are responding and reacting in certain ways, especially in stressful times, will move you along your self-evolution path.

Cultivating regular self-consideration habits can help you have more energy and notice where your energy levels are. Simply recognizing when you are starting to feel exhausted, or when a person or situation is sucking up too much of your bandwidth, are vital skills. When you know what's going on, you have options. You can slow down, pause, and course correct as needed.

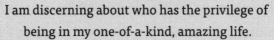

Say It with Me
I am discerning about who has the privilege of
being in my one-of-a-kind, amazing life.

Satisfaction, Joy, and Gratitude

Two emotions that can elevate healthy energy levels are satisfaction and joy. If those sound like states that only other people get to experience, don't despair. You can choose to create and prioritize these feelings in your life, too.

Let's begin by defining what we're talking about when we talk about satisfaction and joy. Unlike happiness, which is a feeling that exists in the moment—*I feel happy when I see my bestie, then not so happy when I'm stuck at home with a cold*—satisfaction speaks to a more enduring state of being content and fulfilled. We can feel satisfied with our choice of partner or our chosen path. Joy, too, is distinct from situation-dependent happiness. It contains exuberance and can arise spontaneously. Being in a state of joy feels amazing.

So, how can you invite more satisfaction and joy into your life?

First things first: pay attention to the quality of your relationships, as they are a huge determiner of your satisfaction.

So, take an inventory of your close relationships. Are there certain bonds that could be healthier? If so, consider how they could improve. This might mean identifying and addressing issues that you've let slide in the past, for example, calling your partner out if they start slacking on their share of the domestic tasks that keep your family life humming along.

You can use your four-step proactive boundary plan from chapter 8 (see page 175) to begin to effectively resolve conflict and set your desired boundaries. One HFC client with a challenging sibling chose to connect with her brother only on "safe" topics such as sports, the weather, and his kids. This was more satisfying to her than having the same argument about politics over and over.

Satisfaction also increases when we're able to share our unique gifts and talents. I frequently see clients who have shiny, impressive titles but are wildly unfulfilled because what they are doing is not their passion. Just because something looks good on paper doesn't mean it fills up your cup. When it comes to creating satisfaction, it's key to carve out time for activities that light you up. One of my HFC pals was missing her dancing days when she got an idea. With an attitude of experimentation, she wondered why she couldn't just rent a dance studio and invite another dance-loving pal to join her? They found a gorgeous studio, brought flowers to make the space feel like a celebration, and curated a playlist in advance. One of their other friends asked if he could shoot photos, and they said, "Why not?" The whole point was to enjoy themselves in the spirit of play—that's it. My pal did not turn into a professional dancer by any means, but this experience taught her the power and value of seeking joy.

Joy feels good. You don't have to wait for it to spontaneously arrive to cultivate the feeling it gives you viscerally. When you bring joy to mind, notice the sensations in your body. For me, there's a lightness in my chest; it's almost like my heart is smiling. Noticing what it feels like for you can help you become more mindful and joyful—you imprint it on a cellular level, which absolutely will give you the power to bring more joy into your life.

BACK TO YOU
Fill Your Cup

To tap into your sense of creativity and play, consider a fun idea that you can green-light. Here are some suggestions to start you off:

☐ Start an herb, flower, or vegetable garden.

☐ Invite friends to join you in volunteering with Habitat for Humanity.

☐ Break out some old music and have a listening party with a friend.

☐ Surprise your partner with their favorite chocolate cake, just because.

What is the first thing that comes to mind? Are there certain activities that you've wanted to do more of that bring a feeling of happiness, or even joy?

Whatever your mind landed on, pour more attention into that activity over the next month.

Think about this more like an experiment than a homework assignment. Make your life a learning lab and get out there to see how it feels when you're consciously pursuing and cultivating more satisfaction and joy.

It may seem counterintuitive, but when you prioritize cultivating joy, some old stuff might come up for review, especially if you experienced childhood abuse or neglect. You may feel fear, guilt, or shame, and where there's shame, we are also prone to blame (ourselves or others). If you find yourself grappling with any of these feelings, pay attention and get curious about the cause. Use the 3Qs for Clarity (see page 148) to journal it out and see what's revealed.

> ### *Loving Reminder*
> It's never too late to create the life
> and relationships you desire.

In shifting out of sticky feelings, gratitude helps. Turn your dial toward what you are sincerely grateful for. You may even have an easier time accessing your gratitude in times of stress and struggle. One of my clients, in the middle of a family medical emergency, started bawling when a worker at the hospital cafe gave her a free ginger tea. The worker then came out from behind the counter, and said, "Let's pray for your relative." This simple act of kindness touched her deeply. But you don't have to wait until you're on your knees to find and express your thanks. Consider writing down three things you're grateful for right before you go to sleep. This helps to reframe your perspective, no matter how the day went.

Falling Back into Old HFC Behaviors

What happens to all our progress and good self-care work when there's a crisis? Just like with any recovery experience (and just like I did with my mother's cancer), we may slip into old behaviors and reactions. Case in point: recently my son and his family were driving to visit us for a holiday weekend when they broke down on the side of a busy highway. As soon as I got the text, I was very concerned and immediately jumped into action. I called my mother to see how far my cousin lived from where they were stranded. I started quickly googling to find a nearby car rental spot for them. I texted my sister to find a Honda dealership in their vicinity. I finally spoke to my son, who was understandably frustrated by this turn of events. But when I told him I'd spoken to the car rental dealership nearest him, he said, clearly and quickly, "I did not ask you to arrange for a rental car." He was right. He had already handled it all. I could have simply asked him if there was anything I could do to help before I started my frantic SOS calls. It was a momentary step back into an active HFC reaction.

If you find yourself in a similar situation in your recovery, there are two questions to consider before you take action for someone else: *Did they ask you to?* and, *Do you have their consent?* If the answer is no, that's the time to step back, pause, and use your self-care habits to replace your compulsive need to fix, give, control, or otherwise interfere. Your muscle memory will kick in (as mine did), and it will be easy and natural to get back on the right track.

Remember: progress, not perfection.

There are a variety of challenges that will test our recovery. A loved one may become sick, or work might be super taxing and our nerves extra frayed. Stressful world events can also bring up intense feelings that tempt us back into our old ways. In these out-of-sorts times, the familiarity of our over-investing and over-functioning can lure us back. This is not uncommon. Relapsing into HFC-ness is actually normal. It is a humble reminder that transforming deeply ingrained behavioral patterns is a lifelong process. It just means we are human. You can simply acknowledge the slip and keep moving forward.

When my mother started cancer treatment and I relapsed to HFC behaviors, I was lucky to have my sister Katie to point out that my mother was in Jenna's capable hands. That was the wake-up call I needed to go back to basics. I called my niece to ask her if she could manage my mom's schedule-of-care calendar. She was more than happy to take that on. In my work, I delegated certain tasks to my team, which created more time for hiking with Vic. Asking him for help was huge, too. He was empathetic, sitting with me and listening as I got real about the deep fears my mother's health crisis had sparked in me. He witnessed me with compassion and love, and that, too, was a reminder to be more compassionate and considerate toward myself.

> ### Say It with Me 💬
> I prioritize my self-care and self-consideration
> with excitement and ease.

Have Compassion for Yourself

Self-compassion is a critical component of a solid self-care foundation. We're human. We're going to fall off course and be imperfect and auto–advice give and do all the things we once swore we'd never do again. It's okay. With self-compassion, you can tend lovingly to the whole gamut of feelings that might be coming up in times when you're activated. If old shame creeps in, let self-compassion remind you that you are not a bad person for reverting to a familiar coping mechanism. Some part of you was reaching for comfort, and that intention to soothe is not a bad thing. You can now choose different ways to self-soothe. Your self-awareness and track record of working to make these changes in your life is something to be proud of. One backslide does not a "failure" make.

When you begin to fix the HFC-ness of your behaviors, you regain a *ton* of bandwidth. You still know how to get stuff done like a boss, only now your conscious choices and self-care make it possible for you to apply this high-functioning capability to more constructive ends, like your personal goals and dreams. You can now leverage your high-functioning ways as a superpower, applied mindfully to the creation of your dream life.

After my mother's treatment was completed, she came to live with Vic and me for twelve weeks. In a way, having to focus on my self-care while Jenna was living with her ended up making the time she spent with us much more meaningful and enjoyable. I always love being with my mother, but it was the return to *my* center that made it possible to be fully present and so deeply appreciative of the village of loving family folks and friends who made it all possible. Fortunately, she returned to full health and is currently feeding her birds, going to church, weeding her rock garden, and being as bossy as ever.

As uncomfortable as the inevitable backslides can be, the discomfort is short-term. Remember to keep self-care and self-consideration at the forefront of your efforts and keep your eyes on the prize of your long-term personal evolution. It's always worth it.

▶ TAKE ACTION ◀

- **Top of Mind.** Reflect on your day with a focus on self-consideration. Ask yourself: Did I make choices today that were truly in line with my preferences, needs, and values? Did I prioritize my well-being? This will gauge how often you consider your needs and encourage you to make more self-considerate decisions.

- **Take Care.** Perform a quick, clutter-clearing spree in a small area of your home or workspace. Organizing your external environment can bring a sense of internal calm.

- **Go Deeper: Create a Morning Routine.** Creating a strong foundation for your day is essential for HFC recovery. Dive into your morning routines on page 248 in the "Go Deeper" section at the back of the book. Discover how the first few hours of your day can set the tone for expansion and success.

CHAPTER 10

Surrender

AT THIS POINT in our journey together, we're celebrating *you* and the healthy choices you've started to make. We're also celebrating the healthy life you'll continue to make as you shift from *too much* to *just right*. We're celebrating the *aha moments*, both large and small—those moments of realizing, *damn, my own side of the street looks good!* When we stop feeling responsible for others' feelings, decisions, and outcomes, we learn to take responsibility for our *own* decisions and feel our *own* feelings. Then we can really bask in the beauty, joy, and fun of what *is*. Life can be magical. Life *is* magical. And that beauty and magic increase exponentially when we reclaim our unique energy and bandwidth—when we reclaim our life.

Liberation from HFC tendencies can be very powerful and very poignant. A few years ago, my pal Kendra attended an event where I was teaching about high-functioning codependency and the importance of boundaries. Three months later, she told me that the concepts she learned in my session clicked with her so deeply that she had a visceral, life-changing response.

"I felt like I'd been 'the Man in the Iron Mask' for forty years, then I got a key and could take the whole thing off." Kendra, a singer, songwriter, and podcast host, had been intensely focused on her own growth and development for years. She had a young daughter and wanted to "get right" with herself so she could be a better parent. She knew she had entrenched patterns of seeking validation and approval from others. "I had wanted the *whole world* to cosign that I was worthy and that they loved me and approved of me. This codependency was taking up eighty percent of my energy. Suddenly, without that, all this space opened up."

What struck me about Kendra (and you may relate to this, too) is that she was already emotionally exhausted from how she had been relating *forever*, but it was seeing herself, for the first time, in the high-functioning codependency description that allowed her to recognize the key to taking off her iron mask.

I've seen shifts like this time and time again in my practice and courses—women having the realization: *Oh, my god, there is a better way.*

By tuning in to yourself (and no longer self-abandoning), you uncover your very own treasure map to your healing and liberation. Like Kendra, you, too can have a game-changing pivot that leads you to act way less codependently. You, too, can discover better ways of being and observing yourself in the world and within.

New Rules of Engagement

HFC recovery is about seeking mutuality in relationships and allowing life to flow more naturally. This means ditching our hyper-independent streak, tempering our auto-advice and fix-it instincts, and learning to listen without offering judgment or a corrective fix. As we established in chapter 4, solid relationships are built on *interdependency*, where each person can rely on the other and feel free to negotiate for their own needs, desires, limits, and preferences. As you create a fundamental trust and respect that goes both ways, you will feel relieved to not be doing it all. You're in it together, with different strengths and skill sets. Neither person puts themself in the position of manager; both are managing themselves and respecting the sovereignty of the other.

In practice, interdependency is a healthy form of dependency that strengthens relationships. It is refreshing to slow down and be more mindful about how you're relating to yourself and the other person.

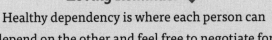

Loving Reminder 🖤
Healthy dependency is where each person can depend on the other and feel free to negotiate for their own needs, desires, limits, and preferences.

Practicing the Most Generous Interpretation (MGI)

As we've been exploring, being judgmental or controlling diminishes the quality of our relationships. While it might be understandable (and human) to, at times, leap to a harsh conclusion, we know it's not going to help us get to know the people in our lives better. Dr. Becky Kennedy, a clinical psychologist and author of *Good Inside: A Guide to Becoming the Parent You Want to Be*, has helpful guidance for parents that can apply to all relationships. To step out of the judgment zone, look for the Most Generous Interpretation (MGI) of someone's behavior instead of the Least Generous Interpretation (LGI). In Kennedy's view, looking through this more generous lens will help you see the good inside the other person, even if their behavior might be questionable (or, questionable according to *you*). For example, let's say that your spouse failed to call you when they landed at the airport. The LGI might sound something like, *I can't believe it, they're always so inconsiderate. They know how stressed I get when they fly so their "forgetting" means they must not care.* If you have ever been in a similar scenario, well, you know how well that conversation is going to go when you approach your spouse with this mindset. The MGI, on the other hand, might sound something like, *I wonder what happened. We just talked about this. I'll wait to speak with them and hear what's going on. They might have had a work call.* If you express the MGI, that conversation will be far more productive.

Staying Curious

When you approach any kind of uncertainty with curiosity, you're also creating more room for compassion and acceptance (including self-compassion). It took me time to learn this.

One weekend at the Chopra Center I was introduced to the concept of *yum-yucking*, by the late Dr. David Simon, the founding medical director of the Chopra Center and a world-renowned neurologist and expert in mind-body medicine. Yum-yucking is when we're sitting in constant judgment, approving and disapproving, liking and disliking, in a revolving door of commentary. Hearing this, I immediately realized, *Oh, man. I am such a yum-yucker!* This helped me to slow down and notice when I felt myself going headlong into judgment and control. After this experience and observing this in my clients, I feel confident saying that HFCs have a special ability to yum-yuck all day long (even if we only think it!). We can be the Judge Judys of our friends, family, and, well, the world, thinking or saying things like:

Love that skirt, but the boots have to go.

Congrats on the job, but that's gonna be a long commute.

So happy you are in love, but long distance rarely works.

. . . and so on.

Dr. Simon's point was that the yum-yucking takes up a lot of mental bandwidth. When we begin to notice we're doing it, we can open up to a more expansive perspective, and get curious about our own observations and judgments. We can create space in our minds to accept others, and when we give them that acceptance, it's a whole lot easier to give it to ourselves as well.

It was during this weekend that I started to realize how much my judgments and beliefs were stand-ins for a healthy sense of identity. Who would I even be if I wasn't silently casting judgment on random people? It's almost as if, in the yum-yucking of it all, I was insulating myself against having to be scared by all the uncertainty that surrounded me (because, hey, that's life).

Judgments make us feel like we're in control, but this is an illusion. The *only* constant in life is change. So, when we make quick assessments of whose marriage is going to fall apart or get downright indignant over which streaming service is superior, we are not staying open or furthering our growth as human beings. We're merely *pretending* we're safe from change.

Judge Judy-ing the crap out of our lives and relationships can be where genuine compassion ends. Our strong attachments to our judgments, opinions, and beliefs do not contribute to the healthy development of ourselves, either. So, learning to let go of them and not overly identify with them can be freeing. Learning to be more open to this reality, while remembering that every person is on their own path, helps us to adopt a more generous and open lens. Everyone has their own lessons and preferred way of doing life. When we cultivate a more friendly relationship with this truth, we all win.

The following are a few tried-and-true principles for overcoming yum-yucking, practicing MGI, fostering mutuality, and supporting our own growth.

Open, Empathic Listening. Needing to manage the flow of a conversation is similar to feeling overly responsible in relationships. When we are routinely filling in silent moments or dictating the direction of the conversation, our friend or loved one may not have the space to fully express themselves, which means we may never learn truly important things about them. Similarly, being a present conversationalist can be challenging if we're preoccupied with managing how the other person feels, rather than simply being present to what they are sharing and our *own* words and feelings.

Healthy, open communication is being able to hear what someone else is expressing and to empathize, without judgment or auto-advice giving. The next time a pal, loved one, or coworker comes to you with a problem, practice saying, "That sounds like a lot. How can I best support you now?" or "I feel you. This seems hard." You can approach your interactions not as the resident therapist, coach, or strategist—nor as a nonstop chatterbox anxiously filling the space—but as a caring friend, partner, or family member. It might feel a bit unnatural at first, but the more you do it the more natural it becomes.

Affirm the other person's essential right to make their own decisions. For example, you could say, "I trust that you know what's right for you. I believe in you." If they press and want to ask your opinion, refrain from jumping in and instead take the opportunity to say, "I'm happy to share my two cents, but what's most important is how you feel and what your thoughts are on this. What does your gut say?"

By taking a warm but less directive approach, you are showing that you value the other person's feelings, intuition, and desires. You get to be *a part of their solution*, without overstepping their boundaries. And in the process, you come to know and understand them better.

BACK TO YOU
Ask Expansive Questions—Then Listen

Below is a list of expansive questions that you can use to encourage open listening. Take a moment to say them out loud and see how they feel.

☐ "What does your gut instinct say?"

- "How do you feel about that?"

- "Could you tell me a bit more about that?"

- "Is there more you want to say about that?"

- "Is there anything else you'd like to share?"

- "I'm sorry you're going through that."

- "What a crappy situation to be in. I'm sorry."

- "Can you tell me what you need right now?"

- "I'm not sure what to say right now, but I'm here to listen."

- "Thank you for sharing this with me."

When you practice being present instead of jumping in with a fix, a judgment, or an opinion, you empower others to find their own way, and you cultivate depth and trust in your relationships.

Be Flexible. Life happens. While things not going according to plan may have been your worst nightmare pre-HFC recovery, now you're better served by embracing unexpected events as much as you can. Stepping outside the box and getting creative—or simply laughing when circumstances become absurd—can be healthy and healing for you and the people you're in a relationship with. A downpour on the day of your garden wedding? Not ideal but, hey, Mother Nature has a mind of her own and you can roll with rain. One of my HFC clients who managed events at her busy corporate office had one important dinner where *everything* went wrong. Instead of freaking out and getting into hyper-control mode, as would have been her usual HFC tendency, she'd had enough therapy to think, *maybe there's a good story in this ridiculousness.* Her light attitude set the tone and while things were not perfect, everyone had an amazing time and ended the night feeling stronger as a team.

Acknowledge Your Mistakes and Authentically Apologize. Healing from HFC-ness means letting go of the need to be perfect. You are human and not above reproach, just like everyone else on this planet. Being thoughtful and admitting when you are wrong will make your relationships better, no question. That might mean saying, "I'm really sorry I cut you off when you were talking about your friend's car accident. It was insensitive. Please finish the story." Leave them room to respond to your apology; when you don't, you've shifted back into control mode.

Prepare to Disappoint. Another aspect of embracing your humanity is accepting the reality that there will be times in your life when, in order to do what's right for you, you must disappoint someone else. When we actively attempt to avoid disappointing others, we set ourselves up for pain, resentment, and, ironically, more disappointment. A part of your HFC recovery is changing the lens on this. When you can look at disappointing others through the lens of taking care of yourself first, you create space to do what's right for you. You may also discover that your relationships are more resilient than you think. This also holds true for feeling disappointed about the choices and decisions of others.

Author, empowerment coach, and podcast host Mel Robbins created the simple but brilliant, "let them" protocol. When you "let" others do whatever it is that they are about to do, it creates emotional peace for you and less judgment about the people in your life. Simply say to yourself, *let them*, as a way to release the desire to control, and as a healthy reminder to hightail it back to your own side of the street.

Accentuate the Positive. Generosity is important in any relationship. If you find yourself unable to muster any goodwill, take a step back and consider what the other person does well. This helps you move out of judgment mode and into a more encouraging and positive mindset. In cases where the other person's shortcomings press your buttons, look within to understand why you are so bothered. This will help you engage with a clear heart and mind. It will also help you learn to accept that, hey, we all have shortcomings. Note that when I say "shortcomings," I'm not talking about behavior that is abusive or unacceptable to you.

Don't Assume. The chronic HFC struggle with disordered boundaries and poor communication skills can be a breeding ground for assumptions and unspoken expectations. Continuing to foster open, honest communication means that your requests and desires are transparent and vocalized. When you move from "I shouldn't have to say this," or "I thought it was obvious," to "I'd like to make a simple request," or "Let's be clear about who is taking responsibility for what," you set up your relationships to succeed and yourself to feel seen, heard, valued, and loved.

Vocalize Your True Feelings. If you identify as an empath, you may need some extra mindfulness and practice in this area of refraining from assuming and mind reading. Because empaths naturally sense how the other person is feeling, they tend to react to the emotional pressure within themselves to make sure the other person feels okay. As you continue to register how valid and valuable your own feelings and experiences are, you can move from thinking, *I could never tell them that what they said upset me,* to taking steps to vocalize your true feelings and seek out mutually agreeable solutions.

Proactively Ask for Help. As you continue with your HFC recovery, you'll experience relief and ease as you get past the hurdle of hyper-independence and embrace the two-way street of relational giving and taking. You don't have to do it all yourself. Learning how to ask for help is where the rubber meets the road. I went from being the kind of person who wouldn't even let a taxi driver lift a heavy bag (even though that is part of the job!) to the kind of person who now embraces receiving support and assistance. This might mean planning a potluck for the holiday dinner instead of hosting a three-course meal, or allowing my team to take things off my plate if my energy is better utilized elsewhere. Pre–HFC recovery, when I look back at how exhausted I was *all the time*, it's almost shocking how much I resisted asking for *anything*. Now I'm all about the good vibes that flow *both ways* when I'm vulnerable in admitting that I can't do it all myself—and no longer want to. Having a more balanced give and take is an important component of intimacy, so watch where you're inclined to block help and see if you can instead say, "You know what, I'm underwater with this deadline. Can I ask you to take care of dinner tonight?" Asking for help might also look like letting your guard down and admitting when you're struggling or scared to get support. Ultimately, your recovery is your own, but that doesn't mean you can't be real and vulnerable and allow trustworthy others in.

BACK TO YOU
Say Yes and Accept

Shifting out of HFC-ness means embracing others' generosity. It feels good to help others, as you have no doubt experienced, so don't rob someone else of this gift, either.

Raise your awareness about all the big and small ways that you might be blocking people from adding value to your life.

It could be as simple as the cab driver offering to get out of the cab to come put your bag in the trunk and instead of saying, "No, no, no," saying, "Yes, please. Thanks for offering."

Keep a journal to write notes about your experiences, your feelings, and any realizations that materialize.

While it may take time and practice to feel comfortable with the give and take of interdependence and mutuality, when you get the hang of things, it becomes your new normal. You get a lot more of your time, energy, and focus back. As you mentally prepare for any reactions, focus on your self-care and boundaries. Remind yourself of your rights as a sovereign being. Engage in activities that help you cultivate healthy self-esteem. Normalize asking for help when you need help, or company if you desire company. Rather than get tugged back into the muck that is dysfunctional HFC relating, be fierce about getting your needs met. Tell people when you're not into a plan that inconveniences you and open up a dialogue to find a compromise that feels more equal. Trusting yourself to take care of your own needs will naturally extend outward, helping you trust that others, too, are perfectly capable. As the *It has to be me* and *I know best* illusions fade, in their place, you can embrace a wider world of understanding, connection, and discovery.

> ### *Loving Reminder* 🖤
> When we approach uncertainty with curiosity instead
> of fear, this creates more space for acceptance and
> compassion (including self-compassion).

Changing the Dance

Others are going to notice the changes in you, and no matter what their opinion is, your job is to remain dialed into your *own* needs, feelings, and goals and not get sidelined.

Some folks will appreciate your new assertive, non-meddling self and even admire the guts it takes to switch up the dance. Others, however, may not be so receptive to these changes, especially if you've been in a long-standing relationship dance. The folks who fall in the latter category are most likely fearful of this change and how it will affect them.

Fearing change is human, as we've established. It might show up as resistance and lead to pushback in the form of lashing out, sulking, or passive-aggressive comments and behaviors. One variation on pushback is what Dr. Harriet Lerner deemed "the change-back reaction" in her book *The Dance of Anger*. Here's an example: if you decide that you want to ask for more help around the house (like Dina did in chapter 4), your partner may throw a mini-tantrum or revert to a state of helplessness, even though you both know they're not helpless. With this change-back reaction, the other person is indirectly communicating their disapproval of your new way of operating. This is an unconscious attempt to keep or reinstate the status quo. Prepare yourself ahead of time. Everything we've covered so far in terms of self-care is going to serve you in staying aligned with yourself. As hard as it might be to accept, their reaction and behaviors are theirs to manage. Your job is to keep your focus on holding your boundary and creating a new way to relate. That's how you stay in your own power.

The folks in your life are entitled to their feelings, but getting pushback does not necessarily mean you should abort the mission of changing what's not working. Stay the course and have faith in *you*. Remember, change happens step by step. One small shift at a time, and your HFC recovery will pay off in the form of your future happiness, which includes balanced, healthy relationships.

As you change the dance, it might help to remember that you're going through an awakening and changing unhealthy relational patterns to better ones. As you become healthier, you might start to notice that certain loved ones tell you certain information or news sheepishly, as if they're expecting you to judge them (meanwhile, you've quietly gone on a yum-yucking fast—for life). As you stop managing people and start cultivating more mutuality, it can be very illuminating, as well as humbling, to see where (and with whom) the well-worn traces of your HFC-ness are still in effect. In the case of a loved one anticipating your judgment, the best thing you can do is to show them with your new words and behavior (shown consistently, and over time) that you are fully in support of them living their own lives.

There are going to be times when a family member looks to you for direction on how to navigate a tangled situation and is utterly confused that you've stepped out of your auto-fix-it role. "First, I'd love to hear your thoughts," is an engaged and caring response. Asking expansive questions can also help you here (see page 210). You may still choose to share your thoughts and ideas, but now you can do so mindfully and without feeling responsible for the outcome.

Eventually, all the new dances become second nature. The more consistent you are with boundary-setting and self-care, the more energy and motivation you'll have to stay the course. Stay true to yourself and your word. Before you know it, you will start to see and feel changes in your relationships, as well as how you relate to and nourish yourself.

Loving Reminder 🖤
When you feel like you're swimming
upstream, flip over and float.

Surrender and Peace

At first, "surrender" can feel like a dirty word to HFCs. We pride ourselves on never giving up, always finding a solution, no matter what it takes. As we have covered throughout, the cost of our non-surrendered ways is steep. So, when we talk about making conscious choices, we have to talk about the "how" of surrender. Please understand that I'm not suggesting "surrender" in the sense of waving the white flag and giving up on life. I mean surrendering the responsibilities that are not ours, surrendering to our own humanity, and surrendering to actual reality. Surrender means recognizing what we cannot control, such as what others think of us, or how others behave. It is important to creating peace—and it can be challenging. Whatever relationship or situation is eating up too much of your bandwidth right now, you can learn to let go of anything that's not yours (including others' feelings and choices) and be in the flow of life's larger currents. You deserve to be a main consideration in your own life equation.

For me, one of the hardest parts of the crisis with my sister Jenna that I mentioned in chapter 2 was surrendering to the truth of her situation. Through a whole lot of self-reflection, I learned the difference between what was appropriate for me to handle and what was not. Jenna's sobriety and romantic life was not mine to manage, but my own brand-new domestic life with Vic and the boys absolutely was.

Surrendering to what I *could* do and what I could *not* do was the start of unlearning over-functioning HFC behaviors and learning to control what I could control—namely, what kinds of experiences I allowed for myself. If there was even a remote chance that I could have saved Jenna by continuing to do what I'd been doing, I would have kept doing it. But when Bev pointed out that it was impossible, I also felt an incredible sense of freedom to no longer be responsible.

As an HFC in recovery, I can promise you that the moment you realize that you are truly not responsible for others (besides minor children, of course) will be one of the most transformative experiences of your life. It's freeing, expanding, and humbling, all at the same time. What really helped me to surrender control was getting curious about my own compulsions, giving myself permission to slow down, and asking for help—three things I'd never "had time for" when I was on autopilot as a full-fledged HFC.

You, too, may find yourself summoning plenty of courage and inner grit as you let go of that which you have historically taken on as your own. It may be hard to step back and let your partner hash out their own family stuff. It may be hard to not be the one raising your hand to do the awful, yet imperative, task you're certain no one wants to do (not even you, if you're honest). It may be hard, but trust me, surrender is not as hard as clinging for dear life to something that is ultimately not yours to cling to. The more you live in the truth that you're not responsible for what everyone else is doing, thinking, or feeling, or how they're behaving, the more you'll be opening yourself to the wondrous side of surrender, and a far richer experience of life.

Whatever transcendent force you may subscribe to (God, the universe, nature, etc.), there is something out there that's larger than you, than all of us. When you quit needing to be *the one* to make things happen, truly amazing things can happen. Meaningful coincidences abound when we're open, allowing, and peaceful. Assuming "the surrender pose" creates new possibilities, ones that we never would have come up with on our own.

I had a client whose beloved father was dying of pancreatic cancer and had come to the end of his desire for treatment. At first, she was incredulous, angry, and panicked. She wanted him to fight for himself—and for her. When we were able to unpack what was really going on, she simply didn't want to lose him. Eventually she was able to surrender to the fact that his health choices were his own to make, and she was able to spend ten deeply meaningful days with him in hospice as he transitioned. He died the way he wanted to. Her surrender allowed her to love and respect her father while being present for a sacred experience that she will never forget or regret.

So much of surrender is allowing yourself to be led by your heart and intuition. By now, you have developed some degree of trust in yourself and how you feel inside. The very act of choosing this book is a demonstration of this trust. Some part of you felt uneasy with how you were operating but felt enough hope that you could heal, which led you to spend your precious time reading this book. This trust and connection to what you feel—your heart and your gut instincts—lead you to being in that flow-like surrendered state with an inner sense of peace and calm.

> ### Say It with Me 💬
> After all this time, I realize I am the one I've been waiting for.

Embracing the Unknown

As HFCs in recovery, we will continue with raised awareness about how we are relating to life in general, but especially to the unknown. As we become more emotionally resilient, we can learn to greet uncertainty with curiosity. Recognizing this shift is important because when we don't, we can miss out on the magic of life. As Deepak Chopra tells us, "Relinquish your attachment to the known, step into the unknown, and you will step into the field of all possibilities."

When we fully adopt an open mindset, the universe responds with *synchro-tastic* affirmations, which are sometimes quite incredible. When we are alert to these signs and see that the universe is always conspiring in our favor, we can relax. For instance, instead of jumping in with a fix for someone, you respect their process, express your support, and then, almost like magic, they discover a solution that also opens up new opportunities for their growth.

As you continue on your healing path, your ability to self-reflect will, no doubt, expand and deepen, too. This is exciting. In fact, there's no finish line to reach. You are shifting out of HFC-ness and opening yourself up to a whole new way of life—less codependent, more self-aware, less controlling, and more heart-centered. Knowing, feeling, and living from the core belief that you are not responsible for every last thing is life-changing. Embrace the possibility of joy and fulfillment in having relationships that are not transaction-based, controlling, or management-like, but more heartfelt, accepting, and rewarding for both parties.

The bandwidth that you're reclaiming by cultivating interdependence is going to feel revelatory and revolutionary. Your life will be revitalized and reclaimed. You have taken care of your people with impeccable, unfailing devotion for years, and now it's time to pour that same energy into yourself, for the betterment of you *and* everyone you encounter.

It takes a lot of guts to even *want* to open your eyes, let go of the HFC control you've known, and consider the full range of choices available to you. Doing this personal evolutionary work—taking off your decades-old iron mask—is not for the faint of heart. When the going gets tough, make sure to remember how far you've come and just how emotionally resilient you are. Be patient and kind to yourself, as there are bound to be stumbles along the way. Remember and revere your humanness. Embrace missteps as data points and note your lessons learned. Keep asking to see the gifts in any given situation. When you find yourself stuck in a frustrating circumstance, ask yourself, *What gem of self-wisdom is in this for me?* Set intentions to keep the self-reflection and self-awareness you've gained front and center in your mind, as a reminder of all that you know, all that you are, and all that you can be.

One of the very best parts of recovery is reclaiming your right to joy. (The little kid in you may have been waiting a long time for this moment!) Seek out things that make you laugh, smile, and just simply enjoy what it feels like to be truly present and open to life's wonders.

As an HFC in recovery, you benefit when you can be empathic with yourself and your healing process. There's no gold star, just a slow and steady ease with which you're learning to care for yourself and reorient your entire life perspective. Keep looking for evidence of your strengths, talents, and unique gifts, and use this awareness as the fuel for your motivation to keep moving forward. Remind yourself often of how brave you are, how strong you are, how loving you are, and how capable you are. This is a form of self-compassion, too.

It's my ultimate dream that more and more women recover from high-functioning codependency, ditch the disease to please (and control) others, and start living from a whole different paradigm of authenticity, inner peace, surrender, and flow. This means accepting, embracing, and celebrating yourself exactly as you are. So, continue to honor your feelings without judgment and with a boatload of self-compassion. Slow down regularly to check in and make sure that your relationship with yourself gets all the water and sunshine it needs to truly flourish. One day, you will open your eyes and realize that the shifts have taken deep root within your being, and the way that you engage with the world—and yourself—will truly never be the same again.

▶ TAKE ACTION ◀

- **Top of Mind.** Identify moments where you feel the urge to control outcomes or resist change. In these moments, practice surrender by breathing deep and intentionally releasing the need for control. Allow and accept the situation as it is. This exercise is about learning to become more comfortable with uncertainty and trusting the flow of life.

- **Take Care.** Write down three things you are grateful for. This simple practice of gratitude can shift your perspective and bring a sense of contentment.

- **Go Deeper: Practice Imperfection.** Now is the perfect time to snuggle up in your Zen Den and explore how you can *do* less and *be* more. Go to page 249 in the "Go Deeper" section at the back of the book to get more guidance on overcoming the HFC compulsion to overwork.

Lots of extras online! I created these just for you—find lots of additional tools, strategies, therapeutically designed guided meditations, energy exercises, and many other goodies in the HFC Book Bundle online at hfcbook.com/resources. I'll see you there!

Celebrate

HEALING FROM high-functioning codependency looks different for everyone. But we all benefit from knowing that others have succeeded in changing up their HFC dance. So here I'm sharing a few success stories and key moments in people's shift from *too much* to *just right*. May they inspire you on your journey!

Candice was raised by a Chinese mother and German father, both first-generation Americans who were hyper-focused on academic performance and success. Her mother drilled into her that she had to do everything "perfectly." "Do you know what a 'B' is?" she asked me with a laugh. "A Chinese mother's 'F'!" After attending boarding school and receiving top honors at Harvard, Candice took her over-functioning, self-abandoning HFC self into a career at a big finance company, working inhuman hours. She only took two days off a year for five years until she met her husband. But she took her HFC-ness into family life too. She proceeded to have five kids in six years—meaning she was pregnant or breastfeeding for eight years straight. Finally, she hit a wall. The price to "get it all done" was total self-neglect, turning her into a walking zombie. She realized that on the other side of her high-functioning codependency was being present and feeling alive, and that became her goal. She embarked on a journey of real self-care, healthy boundaries, and self-reflection. Today she is a wellness leader, sponsoring retreats for burned-out executives and exhausted mothers alike. She is living her passion with the full support of her husband and family. Even her mom approves!

Carla, a podcast listener and self-identified recovering HFC, emailed to thank me for my HFC work and to share her story. At 58, she boldly stepped forward for the first time to reclaim her peace. The catalyst was a frightening outburst by her husband at their daughter's wedding—a time meant for joy. Driven by recent insights into her own behavior, Carla recognized the crucial need to respond thoughtfully, breaking her old habit of impulsively excusing his actions. Carla took three days to compose herself. With clarity and determination, she confronted her husband. Speaking with a calm yet firm voice that even surprised herself, she expressed how his actions at the wedding had instilled fear in her, a feeling she was no longer willing to accept. Carla outlined her nonnegotiable boundaries: he needed to seek counseling, re-engage with their church, and build a supportive network. If he failed to meet these, she would leave. This wasn't just about setting boundaries with consequences; it was about demanding the respect and safety she deserved. Her decisive stand shifted the dynamics of their relationship dramatically. It wasn't merely about ensuring a safer, healthier environment but also about demonstrating to herself and her children the importance of self-respect and the courage to enforce change.

Lynn was a beacon of success, but beneath her achievements laid a heavy burden of familial expectation. Since childhood, after her father left, Lynn had become the primary caregiver and eventual financial provider for her family. Her mother viewed her as a limitless resource, fostering a dynamic of resentment as Lynn's relationship with her mother centered around financial support. Determined to redefine their relationship, Lynn set a firm boundary. She offered to buy her mother a property within a budget she defined, presenting her with options for modest condos. Her mother initially rejected these, unable to accept a smaller dwelling. Despite the setback, Lynn stood firm, prioritizing her own mental and fiscal well-being over fulfilling unreasonable expectations. She let her mother know that if she wanted something outside the budget, she would need to buy it for herself. Their relationship tensed, but in time and unbeknownst to Lynn, her mother purchased a modest condo with her own money. When Lynn eventually visited, she found her mother had renewed energy and motivation. She not only accepted her new circumstances but embraced them with pride. And for the first time in a long time, she thanked Lynn, saying, "You're the only person who ever loved me enough to believe I could do it on my own." Their relationship transformed from dependency to mutual respect and autonomy, bringing both women newfound joy and freedom.

Margaret, a participant in my HFC course, recently relocated across the United States for a job that initially seemed promising. However, upon starting, she quickly realized the reality fell short of what was promised. Her boss had set unrealistic expectations and offered compensation that didn't reflect the work demanded, leaving her disappointed, confused, and underpaid. The misalignment created significant anxiety for Margaret, highlighting that the position was a poor fit. As a recovering HFC and people pleaser, standing up for herself was a formidable challenge, but Margaret found empowerment through learning about boundary setting. This newfound knowledge helped her gain the courage to schedule a meeting with her boss to advocate for her needs. Ultimately, she made the difficult decision to leave the job. The experience reinforced the importance of asserting her right to course correct or change her mind and reminded her that it's okay to disappoint others in favor of managing her own well-being.

After a former client, Kylie, lost her father, she intentionally let the pile of condolence cards go unopened on her kitchen counter. Pre-HFC recovery, she would have prioritized immediately responding and answering the many messages. For a consummate do-er like herself, Kylie felt tremendous relief in permitting herself to simply be with her own emotions. It had a positive ripple effect too—

she gave herself more self-care, more self-consideration, and more self-love in processing her father's death.

An HFC pal, Zoey, had a complicated pregnancy that ended in an emergency C-section. She and her baby made it through the operation fine, but afterward, she was devastated to learn that she could not pick up her newborn son for six weeks while her incision healed. She was panicked and upset—this wasn't how she envisioned the first few precious weeks of motherhood. She had many beliefs about the best way to bond with her newborn and had been practicing and preparing for months. Being forced to give up an important part of early motherhood was painful. But because she couldn't lift the baby, her husband took over this crucial role in the family, and this had a transformational effect. At first, she watched his every move, scrutinizing everything. But as she saw him change diapers, prepare bottles, and soothe the baby at night, she gained a newfound respect for him in this unfamiliar realm. Sure, she already saw him as a loving husband and ambitious person, but now she saw him as a capable and devoted father too. Because she couldn't over-function or manage him—she couldn't push him out of the nursery or grab the baby—she gave her husband the space to be himself. From that moment on, she truly considered him an equal co-parent on their parenting journey. Her limitation became the catalyst for their relationship to exist with full mutuality and equability.

Each of these women learned in their own way—and on their own timeline—how to embrace the process of change and, as a result, experienced greater ease, peace, flow, and overall life satisfaction. This can be your reality, too. Spend some time breathing life into a new vision for yourself, one where you feel self-trusting and in control of your side of the street, no longer concerning yourself with the whole damn neighborhood. Surrender to the flow of what *is*, allowing life to reveal its innate wisdom as you develop yourself and create more space and expansion to live a life that's full of authenticity, freedom, and joy.

Go Deeper

THE EXERCISES in this section are essential for healing HFC. Each one helps you integrate your understanding of your relational patterns and guides you to develop the skills necessary to put your knowledge into action. To explore additional tools and strategies or to download and print these, check out the HFC Book Bonus Bundle at hfcbook.com/resources.

CHAPTER 1:
When Doing *Too Much* Is Really Too Much

CODEPENDENT RELATIONSHIP QUESTIONNAIRE

As we now know, codependency does not exist exclusively in romantic relationships; you can be codependent with friends, siblings, coworkers, and even your boss. Raising your awareness of your behaviors is always step one of transformation (because you can't change what you're not aware of).

Put a check next to the statements below that resonate most with you.

Reactive Rather than Responsive (being in a state of anxiety or fight, flight, or freeze)

☐ *I become easily defensive if I feel I am being criticized.*

□ *I am unable to calmly listen to what the other person is saying without reacting like I am guilty of something.*

Porous Boundaries (feeling like you are merged with other people, making it difficult to know where they end and you begin)

□ *I feel responsible for "fixing" what's wrong in someone else's life.*

□ *I often say yes when I want to say no.*

Low Self-Esteem (feeling like you're not good enough)

□ *I often compare myself to others and feel worse as a result.*

□ *I tend to attract and try to "save" people who are hurt, damaged, or suffering in order to feel valuable.*

Dysfunctional Communication (avoiding directly communicating if you think the other person will be angry or upset)

□ *Rather than saying, "I don't like that," I act like it's okay, or go silent to avoid conflict.*

□ *I engage in passive-aggressive communication, or use sarcasm, or silence, or say I'm fine when I'm not.*

Dependency (needing another other person's approval or love to feel okay about yourself)

□ *I'm not okay unless other people are okay.*

□ *I seek the approval of others before I make decisions for myself.*

Fear of Being Alone (feeling lonely or down if you are not in a relationship and feeling energized through your interactions with other people)

☐ *Even when I know a relationship is bad, I stay to avoid being alone.*

☐ *I am highly attuned to the shifting feeling states of others.*

Fear of Intimacy (simultaneously seeking and fearing deep connections)

☐ *I fear judgment, rejection, or criticism in any intimate relationship.*

☐ *I fear if I allow myself to be intimately known by revealing my true self, the other person might reject me.*

Denial (denying the obvious problems in a dysfunctional relationship)

☐ *I make excuses for the bad behavior of others.*

☐ *I feel like my life is happening to me as opposed to me making conscious decisions.*

For a deeper dive, please choose 3–4 of your checked answers to journal about, including how you felt before, during, and after.

IDENTIFYING CODEPENDENT BEHAVIORS

This exercise helps you get clear about where any codependent behavior patterns exist so you can start building healthier, appropriate, and more equitable relationships.

Read the questions below to see what you relate to:

In relationships:

- Are you unable to find satisfaction in your own life outside of a particular person?

- Do you recognize deeply unhealthy behaviors within your relationship but stay anyway?

- Do you support your partner at the expense of your own emotional, financial, mental, or physical health?

- Do you have a habit of keeping close tabs on where your person is and what they are doing?

- If you're in a great mood and your partner comes home cranky, do you suddenly focus on lifting their mood in any way you can, thereby sacrificing your great mood?

At the office or in your work:

- Do you gossip?

- Do you get sucked in to the drama of others, such as talking to another person about a third person who isn't there (triangulation)?

- Do you often do more than your share of the work and end up feeling resentful or underappreciated?

- Do you ever do work that is not yours or cover for others?

- Do you do things you are not asked to do?

With your children:

- Do you do more for your child than what is age-appropriate or healthy?

- Do you do things for your adult children that they can and should be doing for themselves?

- Are you afraid to let your child fail or experience consequences for their choices?

- Deep down, do you fear your child's rejection? Does it ever impede your ability to guide or appropriately discipline them?

With your family of origin and/or friends:

- Are you the advice-giver?

- Do you get angry or hurt when the person doesn't take your advice?

- Are the roles of giver and taker well-defined in your friendships?

- Do you feel resentment for always doing and giving more?

- Do you ever feel used or question the other person's ability to actually care about you?

The more yes answers you have, the more codependent your behavior is within that type of relationship. Use these questions to inform where you need to focus your attention.

CHAPTER 2:
Caring vs. Codependent

CARING OR CODEPENDENT EXERCISE

As we covered in chapter 2, there can be a fine line between being caring and being codependent. If you've ever wondered if your kindness, interest, and support for others is truly caring, or if your "helping" is tipping into codependency, this is your opportunity to find out.

Use this cheat sheet to discern the differences.

SOMEONE WHO IS BEING CODEPENDENT...	SOMEONE WHO IS BEING CARING...
Feels the need to be "needed" by others.	Helps others in an appropriate way when asked (or after asking if help is wanted).
Ignores their own needs or wants for the sake of others.	Takes care of their own needs first.
Draws a sense of self-worth and identity from helping others.	Listens with compassion (not with the intention to fix).
Feels overly responsible for others, over-gives, and crosses boundaries.	Speaks truthfully and kindly (so, therefore, is trustworthy).
Does things for others that they can and should do for themselves.	Gives freely and consciously.
Covers for the mistakes or bad choices of others.	Respects the rights of others to make their own choices and mistakes.
Harbors feelings of resentment, bitterness, or martyrdom.	Holds others accountable.
Gives with unexpressed strings attached.	Shows empathy, compassion, and support to a friend in need.
Accepts lame excuses for bad behavior or poor performance.	Does their best and expects an honest effort from others.

SOMEONE WHO IS BEING CODEPENDENT...	SOMEONE WHO IS BEING CARING...
Attracts needy/unhealthy people who become projects.	Has healthy boundaries and respects the boundaries of others.

CHAPTER 3:
Your HFC Blueprint: Why You Relate the Way You Do

UNPACKING YOUR HFC BLUEPRINT

This exercise is foundational to your HFC recovery journey. In fact, you began it in the Back to You exercise on page 41 in chapter 2. But that was just a snapshot. Now, it's time to go deeper.

During your childhood, your family of origin had specific rules of engagement that informed the way members related to each other and the outside world. These rules set the stage for how you relate in your personal and professional relationships and with the greater world.

Create some time in your calendar to read the following questions, reflect on your answers, and journal more on what you answered *yes* to. You may want to do this exercise over several sessions to allow your responses and insights to gently unfold.

- Did the adults in your life keep commitments and act responsibly?

- Did you grow up in a strict family structure with extremely high expectations?

- Was bad behavior corrected appropriately (without violence or character assassination)?

- Did your family dynamics revolve around one person's needs or desires, often at the expense of others? (This may include addiction, abuse, poor health, or mental health struggles.)

- How did your parents or caregivers show love for one another?

- Did either of your parents or caregivers regularly over-help, rescue, or enable others?

- Were you praised more for your achievements and helping others than for simply being yourself?

- How did your parents or caregivers resolve conflict?

- Did your family view self-care or setting personal boundaries as selfish or unnecessary?

- Were you conditioned to believe that saying no to others' requests is a sign of failure or selfishness?

- Did you experience childhood neglect or abuse?

- Did you have extremely overprotective parents or caregivers?

- Were your parents or caregivers overly concerned about the way others perceived you or your family?

- Were mistakes allowed and forgiven in your family, or blamed and shamed?

- Did your family celebrate or overly admire self-sacrificial behavior?

- Was there honest and open communication in your family of origin? Were people allowed to disagree with one another?

- Were you often expected to take on responsibilities that were not age-appropriate, or to be the caretaker or peacekeeper in the family?

- What types of coping or numbing mechanisms were modeled by your parents or caregivers?

- How did the cultural or religious beliefs of your family influence the rules, expectations, and behaviors within your household?

- Do your relationship patterns mirror that of your parents or caregivers? How?

By reflecting more deeply on your answers, you will illuminate the way your family related to each other and the outside world. The information you glean from this exercise is the foundation for creating a new healthier relational blueprint!

CHAPTER 4:
HFC Relationships: How You Relate to Others

CODEPENDENCY VS. HEALTHY DEPENDENCY

The goal for any healthy relationship is interdependency. That is, each person has the right and feels free to negotiate for their own needs, desires, wants, and preferences. There is a mutuality of trust and respect. Interdependency in practice is a healthy form of dependency that strengthens relationships.

One of the easiest ways to identify a behavior as codependent is to compare and contrast it to interdependent, healthy behavior. Go through the chart below with one significant relationship in mind. While I've used the word "partner" throughout for simplicity's sake, many of the dysfunctional behaviors listed can be expressed in platonic or familial relationships as well.

The chart helps you to identify where your relationships might need work to go from codependent to interdependent.

CODEPENDENT BEHAVIOR	INTERDEPENDENT BEHAVIOR
I prioritize my partner's needs above my own.	My partner and I respect, understand, and express our needs and make decisions together. We hold each other to the same standards.
My partner and I rarely spend time apart. I feel bad asking for personal or alone time.	We respect one another's need to spend time apart.
I do more of the giving and receive less support or help in return.	My partner and I have a balanced give and take and mutually rely on each other.
We keep having the same problems or the same fight over and over. My partner often denies that there are any problems.	My partner and I are open to healthy change and growth. We periodically check in to openly evaluate our relationship. We seek opportunities to deepen our intimacy and understanding of one another.
I do things for my partner that they can and should do for themselves, encouraging them to remain dependent on me.	My partner and I help each other in ways that promote our individual growth and learning. We support one another while remaining self-sufficient.

CODEPENDENT BEHAVIOR	INTERDEPENDENT BEHAVIOR
I put my partner's interests, goals, and values before my own. It is difficult for me to know or express what I want and need.	I feel free to communicate my needs, wants, and preferences authentically.
It is challenging for me to separate my feeling states and identity from my partner's. I often can feel threatened, hurt, or anxious when our beliefs or opinions differ.	I have a solid sense of my own identity outside of my partner. We each have good self-esteem. We recognize and value each other's feelings, ideas, beliefs, and opinions even when we differ.
I judge myself and my worth by how I relate to others. I tend to look to others for validation of my feelings, interests, opinions, and beliefs. I always ask for advice when I make decisions because I don't trust myself to get it right.	My self-worth comes from within. I know I am valuable just for being me and not because of what I do or do not do for others. I can trust myself to make decisions.
I don't have the support I need. I am not as close as I once was with my friends and family, so there's really no one for me to talk with about how I feel.	My partner and I both have great support systems outside of our relationship, including friends and family members that we trust.
I am afraid of being rejected and abandoned. When criticized, I can get defensive or withdraw. I rely on the approval of others to feel valuable and worthy.	I feel safe and secure in my relationship, and I know that even when my partner is upset with me or is being critical, I still have value.
I have weak boundaries and often say yes when I want to say no. I can be very hard on myself and expect perfection.	I feel comfortable disagreeing with others. I don't feel guilty saying no.

CODEPENDENT BEHAVIOR	INTERDEPENDENT BEHAVIOR
When there is conflict in my relationship, it is difficult to come to a resolution or understanding because one or both of us get defensive. We are stuck in a pattern of blaming and shaming.	My partner and I can admit our own mistakes and be honest with one another to promote both our individual growth and the growth of our relationship.
If my partner is having a bad day, so am I. It feels like it's my job to make my partner feel better or to "fix" it. I identify as a people pleaser.	I sympathize with and deeply care for my partner, but I do not take on their problems or feelings as my own. My worth doesn't come from what I do for others.
Our communication is ineffective. When there is a problem, we often fight about it or avoid having a conversation altogether.	My partner and I have healthy communication. We feel comfortable talking about problems openly. We can hold space for one another and actively listen.
My partner often rationalizes faults, mistakes, or problems, refusing to admit responsibility for his or her actions. I find myself telling half-truths or making excuses for my partner's bad behavior. For example, "Oh, they just had a really bad day."	My partner and I admit when we make a mistake or are wrong and strive to be honest and direct with one another and with others. We make amends and trust one another to take responsibility for any wrongdoing.
I get strength and my identity from my relationship. As difficult as it can be, I feel like I can't live without them.	My partner and I are strong apart and strong together. We know how to work toward a mutual goal, but also how to maintain and work toward our individual goals.
Our relationship is intense. It's either really good or really bad, and seems to cycle between the two.	Our relationship is consistent. We both know what to expect and can trust one another and our commitment.

CHAPTER 5:
Why Narcissists and Codependents Attract

UNDERSTANDING LOVE BOMBING

Love bombing is a behavior that can be difficult to recognize, especially early on in a relationship. It usually starts with overwhelming affection and attention, which can feel like sincere interest and real love, but in fact is a narcissist's way of dazzling and disarming you to gain control over you. Love bombing differs from romantic courtship.

The Cycle

Love bombing is actually just one phase of a cycle of narcissistic abuse. Generally, there are predictable stages to this cycle:

1. *Idealization:* This is the grooming stage where they are creating the narrative around the relationship.

2. *Devaluing:* This is the pivot in the relationship. It usually happens when you're not on board with what the manipulator wants, or if you try to pump the breaks on the acceleration of the relationship. The narcissist can get furious and begin to devalue you. They might criticize you, accuse you of being ungrateful, or insult you.

3. *Discarding:* The threat of the narcissist leaving or breaking up with you is always present. They may threaten to break up with you, or actually follow through.

The Love Bomber

- *In the beginning:* Charismatic, convincing, charming, flattering

- *In the middle:* Dismissive, petulant, demanding, critical

- *In the end:* Withdrawn, cruel, threatening

Remember: this is a cycle. You might experience these three different phases of the narcissist's personality before they circle back to being that *amazing, perfect* person you fell for in the first place. This cycling works to keep you in their control.

The Warning Signs

- *Too much, too soon.* The pace of the relationship is accelerated. The narcissist makes declarations of love and commitment very early, and takes actions quickly to cement your future together (like inviting you to a wedding that's more than a year away). Especially in this beginning stage, the love bomber starts to create a narrative about what your shared future will be like before you even really know one another. The narcissist is typically assured, confident, and charming, lavishing you with praise and attention.

- *They are Boundary Bullies.* During the love-bombing phase, they are typically on their best behavior, so thinking of them as a "bully" might not seem to fit. But a Boundary Bully is someone who disregards your preferences, wants, and needs. In the case of a love bomber, it doesn't matter what you say. For example, they suggest a special dinner on Friday night. You tell them you have plans with your friends, but they make the reservation anyway. They act like they never heard you.

- *Pushback inspires punishment.* If you're in a new relationship and you're wondering if this be too good to be true, all you need to do to find out if this is real love or a love bomber is to assert yourself in a healthy way. Make a simple request about something. State that you would prefer to do something other than what they have planned. If their reaction is to withdraw love, give you the cold shoulder, cut off their affection or attention, that's a red flag.

CHAPTER 6:
The High Cost of Being HFC

THE POWER PIVOT

A part of the HFC recovery process is mourning the way we thought our lives were going to unfold and acknowledging how our HFC ways have impacted our life trajectory. This includes mourning relationships, behaviors, decisions, experiences, and more. This process will look different for everyone.

To pivot into a place of true empowerment we must understand, honor, and process our feelings and experiences. Use the following five steps to clear any emotional debris from the past so you can powerfully move into a future that thrills you.

Step One: Honor and Acknowledge Your Feelings
Everyone goes through times of disappointment, frustration, and anger in response to life events. Avoid minimizing your feelings with thoughts like, "I should be grateful for . . ." Instead, become an observer of your past behaviors and internal experiences. Press pause on external distractions and turn inward.

Make a list of the people, places, things, experiences, feelings, circumstances, and situations that bring up feelings of pain or regret. Use journaling to externalize and process your thoughts and emotions. Try not to judge yourself as you're writing—just do a straight brain dump. Identifying and acknowledging your feelings is the first step to processing them.

Step Two: Be Mindful of Scapegoating

In times of stress, it's easy to displace emotions onto others. Be aware of where you might be blaming others for your feelings or experiences. Acknowledge that you are responsible for your reactions, responses, and choices. This step is about taking responsibility and learning from your experiences.

Step Three: Have Compassion for Yourself and Others

Recognize that you made your past decisions with the level of consciousness you had at the time. Practice self-compassion *and* understanding toward others, too. Look back with curiosity and a desire to know yourself better.

Step Four: Find the Gems

Look for positive insights and lessons in any difficult situations from the past. This is not about forced positivity but about finding genuine personal growth opportunities. Reflect on what you have learned about yourself during challenging times.

Step Five: Keep On Keepin' On

Decide to use your experiences and lessons to shape a better HFC-free future. Focus on your strengths and accomplishments. Keep a list of your achievements and use it as motivation to continue moving forward toward your dreams.

CHAPTER 7:
Becoming Emotionally Resilient

EMOTIONAL INVENTORY

Reflect on where you feel the most amplified or stressful emotions. Identify patterns in your thoughts, your relationships, and your behaviors.

- Are you more emotional at home or at work?

- Are you more emotional around particular people? List them.

- What specific situations make you feel heightened emotions? A work deadline? Social situations?

- Do you get emotional when you know you need to have a hard conversation?

- What are your emotional triggers? Can you identify what sets them off?

- Can you identify the worrisome thoughts that get stuck on repeat in your mind?

- Do you experience misplaced or misaligned emotions like crying when you are actually angry?

- What seems to upset you more than it might upset others?

- Are you very affected by the news or what's going on in the world?

Connecting the dots of your own lived experiences will make it easier for you to effectively manage your emotions. Pick three or four of the questions above that you identified with and explore them further in your journal.

CHAPTER 8:
Establishing Good Boundaries

PRACTICE BOUNDARY SCRIPTS

Stop the "Auto-Yes"

In adult relationships, you don't owe anyone an immediate response. When someone makes a request or feels entitled to your time, energy, and consideration, allow yourself to take a beat. If you can curb the impulse to automatically say yes to things that you really don't want to do, you create the space needed to make commitments that are authentically aligned with your desires. This translates to less resentment, less people-pleasing, and more emotional bandwidth that you can better spend elsewhere.

Give yourself a new rule of engagement: take twenty-four hours before making a decision and committing yourself to something. That way, you get time and space to consider how you truly feel and what you want to do.

Below you will find some simple phrases to buy time when you are making a decision:

- "Thank you. I'll have to check my calendar."

- "I'll need to sleep on that. I've implemented a twenty-four hour decision-making policy. I'll get back to you tomorrow."

- "I want to check with my spouse (or sister, roommate, friend, etc.) before committing."

- "I will need to get back to you on that, but thank you for thinking of me."

Start to say no. Here are some phrases to use:

- "Sorry, I'm afraid I can't."

- "I'm not really into that type of (music, food, outdoor event, etc.) but hope you have a wonderful time."

- "I'd rather not."

- "Thank you for thinking of me, but I am already committed on that date."

Below are a few scripts to gently negotiate for your needs and prioritize your preferences:

- **I would like to make a simple request that** . . . *we take turns deciding where to meet for dinner.*

- **I would really appreciate it if** . . . *you could let me finish my story before sharing yours.*

- **I would be more comfortable if** . . . *we could decide together where to go on our annual family trip.*

- **I thought you should know** . . . *that when you interrupt my story it makes me feel unimportant or that you're not listening.*

- **I wanted to bring this to your attention** . . . *that the last few times we've gotten together, I paid more than my share since I don't drink. I should have said something at the time and will if it happens again.*

- **I need to tell you** . . . *that telling Betty something I shared with you in confidence upset me and broke my trust. Please don't do it again.*

- **I want you to be aware of . . .** *how I feel about our interaction the other night.*

- **I've noticed that when . . .** *we are talking, you're frequently looking at your phone. Can you please put it away while we are talking?*

CHAPTER 9:
Real Self-Care

CREATE A MORNING ROUTINE

A sacred morning ritual is a profound act of self-care and an effective way to set yourself up for success each day. By starting the day with intention, gratitude, and mindfulness, you open yourself up to a world of positive possibilities.

The key to a successful morning ritual is consistency. Your routine could be as brief as three minutes, but doing it daily makes a big difference. It's a statement to yourself and the universe that your well-being and internal peace are priorities.

Your morning ritual should be personal and align with your feelings and preferences. You might consider activities like light exercise, listening to music, or simply sitting quietly with a cup of tea. The objective is to create a routine that feels sacred and beneficial to you.

Below are some ideas you can use to craft your morning routine:

- **Meditation:** Meditation is a cornerstone of many effective morning routines. Whether you are new to meditation or have an established practice, incorporating it into your morning can bring clarity and calm. Even two minutes of meditation can make a difference.

- **Gratitude Practice:** Depending on how much time you have and what feels good, you can write a quick list of big and small things you are grateful for or create a full-on journal devoted to daily gratitude.

- **Reading or Journaling:** Engaging in spiritual or inspirational reading or journaling can also be a part of your ritual. This can be tailored to your preferences, whether it's reading a few passages from a favorite book or pulling tarot cards.

- **Mindful Breathing:** Focused breathing exercises not only enhance lung capacity but also improve concentration and mental clarity. You can start with simple techniques like abdominal breathing or alternate nostril breathing, which are known to calm the mind and balance the body's energy channels.

- **Move Your Body:** Do regular movement that feels good and fits into your life. Start where you are and build from there. If you prefer to exercise later in the day, that works, too. (Personally, I find if I don't do it early, I won't do it at all.)

CHAPTER 10:
Surrender

PRACTICE IMPERFECTION

We all know that perfectionism can suck the joy out of life. There is a subtle art to allowing and even encouraging yourself to be imperfect.

Answer the questions below for clarity on where you could use more balance and less perfection:

- Are you able to relax, or does having free time cause you anxiety?

- What is overworking costing you?

- Are there ever things you do just because they are fun?

- Can you give yourself the gift of doing something fun (but not productive) every day?

- Do you ever leave tasks undone?

- Can you choose to embrace a "good enough" job and see how it feels?

Acknowledgments

WRITING A BOOK is a group effort and *Too Much* is no exception. I am deeply grateful for the incredible support I received every step of the way.

Thank you to . . .

First and foremost, to my one and only, Victor Juhasz, for being my person, my partner, and my passion. Twenty-seven years and you're still the most interesting person I've ever met.

I am grateful to our grown sons, Max, Alex, and Ben, and their beautiful families for inspiring me to strive to be the healthiest version of myself. I love you all so much.

To my yayas and closest pals since elementary school: Donna McKay, Carrie Godesky, Ilene Martire, Cathy McMorrow, Maureen Ambrose, and Denise Perrino for a lifetime of support and unknowingly giving me lots of content for this book since you're ALL HFCs!

To my circle of support, inspiration, and friendship, I am blessed beyond measure: Lara Riggio, JoAnn Gwynn, Patty Powers, Danielle LaPorte, Kris Carr, Gina Ratliffe, Marie Forleo, Danielle Vieth, Christine Gutierrez, Helene Clapps, Daryl Bart, Selena Soo, Emily Hayden, Caroline Hobby, Vanessa Cornell, Emily Fletcher, Vienna Pharaon, Samantha Skelly, Michelle Stampe, and Suzanne Guillette.

To my beloved Team TC for generously picking up the slack over the past year. Special thanks to Tracey Charlebois for being in the foxhole with me for a ridiculous number of hours per day till we got it done. To my ride-or-die right hand, Joyce Juhasz, for keeping us organized and sane and for always having the last eyes on everything.

To my literary agent, Stephanie Tade, and her amazing team for taking care of business.

To everyone at Sounds True who worked tirelessly, including Jade Lascelles and Sara Veglahn. Special thanks to publisher, Jaime Schwalb, for her guidance, patience, and kindness, and for encouraging me to bring this unique material to the world. Deep bow of gratitude to my developmental editor, Joelle Hann, whose insight and skills were essential and so very much appreciated.

Notes

CHAPTER 1:
When Doing *Too Much* Is Really Too Much

As author and podcast host Glennon Doyle says, "When a woman finally
learns that pleasing the world is impossible, she becomes free to learn
how to please herself."
From Glennon Doyle in *Untamed* (New York: Random House,
2020), 56.

We now know that the brain's neural connections—estimated to be
in the ballpark of a whopping one hundred trillion—are formed
and potentially altered anew every single day, thanks to our lived
experiences.
From Catherine Caruso in "A New Field in Neuroscience Aims
to Map Connections in the Brain," Harvard Medical School
News (January 19, 2023), hms.harvard.edu/news/new-field
-neuroscience-aims-map-connections-brain.

CHAPTER 2:
Caring vs. Codependent

Burn writes, "Some types of helping and giving create unhealthy
dependencies and reduce others' self-confidence, competency, and
life skills."
From Shawn Meghan Burn in *Unhealthy Helping: A Psychological*
Guide to Overcoming Codependence, Enabling, and Other
Dysfunctional Giving (North Charleston, SC: CreateSpace
Independent Publishing Platform, 2015), 163, Kindle edition.

CHAPTER 3:
Your HFC Blueprint: Why You Relate the Way You Do

My first book, Boundary Boss, *explored our boundary blueprints.*
> From Terri Cole, in *Boundary Boss: The Essential Guide to Talk True, Be Seen, and (Finally) Live Free* (Boulder, CO: Sounds True, 2021).

Swiss psychiatrist and psychoanalyst Carl Jung asserted, "Until you make the unconscious conscious, it will direct your life and you will call it fate."
> Attributed to Carl Jung: "C.G. Jung Quotes" Goodreads, accessed November 1, 2022., goodreads.com/author/quotes /38285.C_G_Jung.

Dr. Harriet Lerner, one of my heroes and the author of The Dance of Anger: A Woman's Guide to Changing the Patterns of Intimate Relationships, *says, "Our society cultivates guilt feelings in women . . ."*
> From Harriet Lerner in *The Dance of Anger: A Woman's Guide to Changing the Patterns of Intimate Relationships* (New York: William Morrow Paperbacks, 2014), 7.

In his book The Myth of Normal: Trauma, Illness, and Healing in a Toxic Culture, *physician and addiction expert Dr. Gabor Maté offers an illuminating definition of trauma: "Trauma is not what happens to you but what happens inside you."*
> From Gabor Maté in *The Myth of the Normal: Trauma, Illness, and Healing in a Toxic Culture* (New York: Avery Publishing, 2022).

He says, "Fawn types seek safety by merging with the wishes, needs, and demands of others."
> From Pete Walker in *Complex PTSD: From Surviving to Thriving: A Guide and Map for Recovering from Childhood Trauma* (Lafayette, CA: Azure Coyote Publishing, 2013), 122, Kindle edition.

She says, "The intensely painful feeling or experience of believing that we are flawed and therefore unworthy of love and belonging—something

we've experienced, done, or failed to do—makes us unworthy of connection."
From Brené Brown in "The Power of Vulnerability" June 10, 2010, TEDx Houston, YouTube video, 4:40, youtube.com/watch?v=iCvmsMzlF70.

CHAPTER 5:
Why Narcissists and Codependents Attract

When you think about a narcissist, what comes to mind?
From "Narcissistic Personality Disorder," Mayo Clinic, last modified April 6, 2023, mayoclinic.org/diseases-conditions/narcissistic -personality-disorder/symptoms-causes/syc-20366662.

DARVO was coined by Dr. Jennifer Freyd, coauthor (with Pamela Birrell) of Blind to Betrayal: Why We Fool Ourselves We Aren't Being Fooled . . .
From Jennifer Freyd and Pamela Birrell in *Blind to Betrayal: Why We Fool Ourselves We Aren't Being Fooled*, read by A. Savalas (Newark, NJ: Audible Studios, 2013), Audible audio ed., 8 hr., 21 min.

In her early thirties, Freyd suddenly recalled a familial betrayal . . .
From Katie Heaney in "The Memory War: A Daughter's Accusations, and the Foundation Built to Discredit Them," The Cut, New York Magazine, January 4, 2021, thecut.com/article/ false-memory-syndrome-controversy.html.

The Boundary Boss *Bill of Rights below is from my book,* Boundary Boss.
From Terri Cole in *Boundary Boss: The Essential Guide to Talk True, Be Seen, and (Finally) Live Free* (Boulder, CO: Sounds True, 2021).

Dr. Ramani Durvasula, psychologist and author of It's Not You: Identifying and Healing from Narcissistic People, *asks a pointed question about loyalty . . . "Loyalty," she points out, "is not meant to be masochism. Loyalty is not meant to be 'stand around and be taken advantage of.'"*

From Dr. Ramani Druvasula "When does LOYALTY become SELF-HARM?" October 9, 2023, YouTube video, 11:59, youtube.com/watch?v=UbpsighMDtc.

Chapter 7: Becoming Emotionally Resilient

. . . Dr. Shefali Tsabary, where she insightfully pointed out, "One hundred percent of the time . . ."
From Dr. Shefali Tsabary on Instagram Live with Terri Cole, "The Parenting Map LIVE Q&A with @doctorshefali," Instagram video, March 4, 2023, instagram.com/p/CpV1vFIhyZt.
According to Jon Kabat-Zinn, the founder of Mindfulness-Based Stress Reduction (MBSR) training, "Mindfulness is awareness that arises through paying attention, on purpose, in the present moment, nonjudgmentally in the service of self-understanding and wisdom."
From Jon Kabat-Zinn, "Jon Kabat Zinn: Peel Back the Onion," May 28, 2015, Mindful, YouTube video, 2:29, youtube.com/watch?v=ABp9Lxg0_5A.

Chapter 10: Surrender

Dr. Becky Kennedy, a clinical psychologist and author of Good Inside: A Guide to Becoming the Parent You Want to Be, *has helpful guidance for parents . . .*
From Becky Kennedy (@drbeckyatgoodinside), "MGI - Most Generous Interpretation," Instagram video, May 18, 2023, instagram.com/drbeckyatgoodinside/reel/CsYsqAIhtA2.
Author, empowerment coach, and podcast host Mel Robbins created the simple but brilliant, "let them" protocol.
From Mel Robbins, "The 'Let Them Theory': A Life-Changing Mindset Hack That 15 Million People Can't Stop Talking About,"

May 29, 2023, in The Mel Robbins Podcast, podcast audio,
Episode 70, melrobbins.com/podcasts/episode-70.

*One variation on pushback is what Dr. Harriet Lerner deemed "the
change-back reaction" in her book* The Dance of Anger.
From Harriet Lerner in *The Dance of Anger: A Woman's Guide
to Changing the Patterns of Intimate Relationships* (New York:
William Morrow Paperbacks, 2014), 7.

*As Deepak Chopra tells us, "Relinquish your attachment to the
known, step into the unknown, and you will step into the field of all
possibilities."*
From Deepak Chopra in *The Seven Spiritual Laws of Success: A
Practical Guide to the Fulfillment of Your Dreams* (San Rafael, CA:
Amber-Allen Publishing: 2015), 75.

About the Author

TERRI COLE is a licensed psychotherapist and relationship expert based in New York. She is the author of *Boundary Boss: The Essential Guide to Talk True, Be Seen, and (Finally) Live Free*, and *The Boundary Boss Workbook*, and the founder of several programs, including Real Love Revolution, Boundary Bootcamp, and Crushing Codependency.

Before becoming an expert in love, boundaries, and codependency, Terri spent years as a bicoastal talent agent negotiating endorsement contracts for supermodels and celebrities. However, her eventual disenchantment with the world of entertainment led her to make a career change in her thirties and become a psychotherapist and empowerment expert. Her mission is to empower women to lead self-determined, fulfilling lives by mastering healthy boundaries and cultivating vibrant relationships.

Over the past two decades, Terri has worked with a diverse group of clients from stay-at-home moms to celebrities and Fortune 500 CEOs. She has a gift for making complex psychological concepts accessible and actionable so that clients and students achieve sustainable change. She empowers a global community of millions across 189 countries each week through her illuminating videos, articles and blog posts, therapeutic meditations, online courses, and popular podcast, *The Terri Cole Show*.

Recognized as an expert therapist and master life coach, Terri Cole has appeared on popular shows such as *GMA3*, *The Doctors*, and *NBC News Daily*, offering her expertise on a range of mental health and relationship topics. In addition to her television appearances, she has been featured on The Real Housewives and hundreds of podcasts. A sought-after voice in major publications, she has contributed to the *Huffington Post*, *Well+Good*, *Oprah Daily*, and *Shondaland*. Her work and insights have garnered attention in *People Magazine*, the *New York Times*, *Women's Day*, *Glamour*, *Elle*, *Forbes*, *Vogue*, *Cosmopolitan*, *CNN*, and *Self*. Discover more about Terri's impactful work at terricole.com.

About Sounds True

SOUNDS TRUE was founded in 1985 by Tami Simon with a clear mission: to disseminate spiritual wisdom. Since starting out as a project with one woman and her tape recorder, we have grown into a multimedia publishing company with a catalog of more than 3,000 titles by some of the leading teachers and visionaries of our time, and an ever-expanding family of beloved customers from across the world.

In more than three decades of evolution, Sounds True has maintained our focus on our overriding purpose and mission: to wake up the world. We offer books, audio programs, online learning experiences, and in-person events to support your personal growth and awakening, and to unlock our greatest human capacities to love and serve.

At SoundsTrue.com you'll find a wealth of resources to enrich your journey, including our weekly *Insights at the Edge* podcast, free downloads, and information about our nonprofit Sounds True Foundation, where we strive to remove financial barriers to the materials we publish through scholarships and donations worldwide.

To learn more, please visit SoundsTrue.com/freegifts or call us toll-free at 800.333.9185.

Together, we can wake up the world.